BITTERSWEET MEMORIES FROM SOMEWHERE ALONG MY WAY

Mark G. Hinesh

This book is respectfully dedicated to my community,

family and friends.

BITTERSWEET MEMORIES FROM SOMEWHERE ALONG MY WAY

Mark G. Hinesh

Foreword by Martin Hackel

Edited by Brian Flynn and Martin Hackel

Pacific Academic Press

First published by Pacific Academic Press, 2012

ISBN-13: 978-1463796617

ISBN-10: 1463796617

TABLE OF CONTENTS

Page

Appendices

Foreword

It was during our first or second day of college when Mark and I met. We became comfortable with each other at once, undoubtedly because of shared experiences such as having grown up on small Wisconsin dairy farms and attending one room schools. Our childhoods meant we learned to be responsible at a much younger age than did our city peers. Our parents trusted us out of sight to operate large tractors and to finish jobs. We knew we had contributed to our family's livelihood in real ways.

Meeting Mark in his second floor room in Berne Hall, I quickly realized he was verbal and confident. He readily talked about his farm, family, and his expectation to enter the US Army and take part in the Vietnam war. If he didn't talk about his friends who were killed in that war the day we met, he did soon after. Through the four years at St. Norbert, Mark and I became closer, and as roommates we spent lots of time discussing the state of the world. We were both politically conservative, though Mark tended to be more moderate than was I.

Mark stood out in terms of his interest in the military in ways that many of us did not. He set his sights on high levels of leadership in the college Reserve Officers Training Corps and accomplished much of that. He could have avoided military service due to problems with his feet, but petitioned to be allowed in. I knew that he had wanted West Point, but ROTC at St. Norbert College was a worthy albeit, alternate, means to the same goal.

We went to Fort Riley, Kansas together for a six week summer camp, a difficult but satisfying experience. After graduation, while I served in the Armed Services Courier Service in Washington, DC, Mark volunteered for Vietnam not once, but for multiple tours of duty. He was not combat qualified, but sought assignments close to danger because he wanted to contribute more.

After returning from the war Mark was stationed at the Joliet Arsenal where I visited him for an afternoon of talk, plus games of pool and basketball. Over the following years, we communicated and visited frequently. He shared his life at Social Security and much about taking care of his mother and other important issues such as the high school mascot controversy for which he was a community leader.

Not everyone is fortunate in having as a lifelong friend, a person of such high character; and one who is willing to "go out on a limb" to work for the good as he sees it, as I do in Mark. Not only caring for his clients in Social Security, working with the nursing home to get the best care for his mother (and going to battle with them when needed), but being available to me and other friends to listen and care. He now provides direct help to needy elders in his community through home visits and gifts of food and other tangibles. He has being doing this for a long time, and we can agree such unselfishness is rare in today's world.

I recommend the following biography to the reader who will experience much of Mark's life through his own eyes and words. Enjoy !

Martin Hackel

November 2012

Chapter 1

Aims and Aspirations

Numerous times I'd start to write only to stall out. Much of this book has been buried in my soul for decades, in particular since Vietnam, and it has been longing for an honest release. Over the years I have kept diaries and written a number of news articles. Sometimes a recollection of the past would come to mind and I made notes of this. I have used all of those to help me write this book. It is not a complete autobiography or collection of memories. Instead, there are descriptions of major episodes in my life and my most enduring and poignant memories. My aim has been to write an honest, informative and entertaining work, in particular for family and friends, and my community.

I describe my heartland and heritage, my family life, schooling, work and some of my war experiences. I love my homeland and to ensure the reader knows my heritage, Chapter 4, "My Heartland" provides a history of Wisconsin and describes the origins of "America's Dairyland". There is also a contributed chapter, Chapter 9, from a clinical psychologist who works for the United States military. The Foreword has been written by a friend from my college days. These provide useful information and special perspectives about the content of this book.

The Hinesh Farm

I grew up on a fifth generation small dairy farm in Wisconsin. As a small boy, I spent countless hours in machine sheds trying to figure out the mechanical workings of the grain reaper, corn binder, 1893 Keystone International Harvester rake and Superior high-wheeled seeder (grain drill). My expectation was that I would grow up to be a farmer and continue to work our Hinesh farm.

Me, age 4, on the radiator of a McCormick-Deering M. (1948)

There were five generations of Hinesh's who farmed nearly 100 years. I have an original deed showing that Franz Hinesh (Great Grandpa) purchased 80 acres and 20 acres of woods three miles distant in Carlton from Josef Kohout (a Czech name meaning "rooster"). The farm soon parted with one and one-half acres by selling it to Carlton Township for its town hall. When my grandparents married in 1898 (the year of Teddy Roosevelt's charge up San Juan Hill), they were using oxen and large sleds with steel runners to haul firewood and sawn lumber home.

My parents, Arthur and Mildred, married in November 1931 and ownership of the farm was transferred to them. They paid Grandpa Hinesh $7,500 for it. The first month, milk brought in $19 and expenses were over $30. The oxen had long left the scene, and horses had replaced them. Two months after my birth in 1945, a shiny McCormick-Deering M supplemented the horses. One of my first pictures has me, a smiling tot astride the radiator of the "big red machine." The agricultural machinery which had been horse drawn were fitted with poles and hitches to adapt to the "M". Using the "M" was not really an improvement because if you drove much faster than horses walked, the machines broke down.

I kept my desire to continue the Hinesh family business of farming right through to my sophomore year at college, despite knowing the high cost of modernization of it that was needed in the mid 1960's. I think it was because I so loved the Holstein cattle.

My Parents and Family as Social Role Models

Our personalities are formed and shaped by those closest to us in the most formative years of our lives: ages one to nine. During those years we are incredibly influenced in our work ethics, social interactions, moral values, spiritual beliefs, perceptions and treatment of the opposite sex.

Is "Dolly" a terrible sexist chauvinistic term in today's lifestyles? I do not believe it is. Daddy called Mama "Dolly" for just short of 49 years. "Mama is such a Dolly, you are". I heard that "Dolly" word hundreds of times, and always equated it with love and tenderness. It expressed the strong emotions I would use to relate to the woman I wished to marry, my special woman who I've felt so much for over the years.

Most of the married men on my Father's side adored their wife. Uncle George Selner called Daddy's sister "Francie", and though her personality could be mean, to him she was "Everything". She died in 1963 and though he survived her for 20 years, he really no longer lived after he had buried her.

Even "Frank the Dandy" could show great tenderness for "May" (Maime) when he was sober. He could be a wonderful singer and romantic. When he was drunk he changed and was mean and nasty. From him I also learned to be tender and never to let alcohol, womanising or greed destroy a soul mate relationship.

Thinking back on it, my best role model for being a husband was Uncle Steven Skarvan, who married Daddy's younger sister Agatha (Hattie). Steve was an old German schooled type (minus the crankiness) *widda lotta* "ya's" in his speech, with a wonderful work ethic and cheery outlook. The four words "Whatevah ya say, Toots" were his for her alone and he used them more than once every time we visited them. Steve didn't just love Hattie, he worshiped her. In this respect, more than anyone else in my past, Steve reminds me of "me" and how I would relate to the woman I would want to be my wife.

I see Saint Stephen holding the rocks which ended his earthly life. It is one of the stained glass windows at St. Laurence Catholic Church, Stangelville, Wisconsin. For me it evokes memories of Steve Skarvan and his courage and tenderness.

For years, Hattie and Steve came out to our farm most Sundays of the months that weather permitted. Social visits to family and friends on a Sunday were a tradition that persisted longer in rural communities. Mama made her traditional Leghorn rooster or White Rock chicken dinners. Everyone acknowledged that none made chicken like Mama.

Hattie's Steve was not only a "jack" of all trades, he really was a "master" of them all. Like his brother Wencil who had the 80 acres farm above us, there was nothing he couldn't repair and usually he did it for free. So, it was a great pleasure feeding him and his family and to express our gratitude for his help. We always loved sharing their company.

Steve always wanted Dad to tear down our log shack, because in the 1930's and 1940's the Levy family built a two-storey home for only about $1500 and Ervin Sinkula built a fancier one for under S3,000. My parents talked about building a new home but it did not happen. Grandpa Hinesh was opposed to it. He "ruled the roast" and made all final decisions in the 1930's, 1940's and thru the 1950's, even though he no longer had ownership of the farm.

Grandpa preferred the farm life of the late 1800's. No modernizing for him or us. He used to say "You can't eat off a house". "What'll Pa say" was my Dad's most used phrase whenever change or improving things came up.

We had three gardens - sometimes four - on the farm. We had no money to speak of (Pa got $650 a month for milk during the Summer pasture flush), but we owed Lorraine Schmidt $375 harvesting fees. She never figured the free labor Dad, "Bozo" and I gave her spread. In effect, she always overcharged us. A few years later she got multiple sclerosis (M.S.) and declined quickly. In my youth I always wondered if God was punishing her - to quote the Bible, "Oh how the mighty have fallen". Also there were the utilities, tractor payments and bills at the Kewaunee Co-op and at Seyks, (the co-op added molasses and Seyks couldn't so we went there less often). To sum up, after bills were paid; nothing left.

By the time I got my say about how the farm should be run and presented plans to begin modernizing, it was the 1960's and costs prohibited doing much. My dreams of farming died.

Hattie was wonderful to Mama and she and Bela String helped save Mama's life when Mama nearly died giving birth to my sister Marie in the Fall of 1936. Acting as midwives, they wonderfully nursed Mama back to health. When the subject came up to have another child to replace my brother Donald Arthur who had lived only two months, they quietly encouraged my folks to go ahead in spite of the risk. Hattie and Bela were both there again to help. So, almost ten months later, and against medical advice, I came into the world and the circle of life was completed.

There are many memories I can vividly recall. There are Aunt Hattie and Uncle Steve being the near perfect couple, stories about Hattie working together on the farm with Mama during the 1930's, and Steve and Frank Kibtzing in their Sunday's finest attire. These were moments of happiness I remember well. They are gone forever. It makes it so hard for me now.

At Christmas in 1956, I took my first model ship, the Seaplane Tender, *Norton Sound*, to show Uncle Steve. He worked as a welder at the shipyards in Mantiowac, Wisconsin. He said "Bring it to the shipyards (where he worked as a welder in Manty) and show them all how well it has been built".

My parent's 25th Anniversary (1956)

Growing up on the Farm

A child's life growing up on the farm is full of learning activities. There were many chores to do. As I got older I progressed from helping to feed the cows and to harder work like milking them, and to completely assuming many of the more difficult tasks. The farm can be a dangerous place with its heavy machinery, such as feed-grinders tractors, and other pieces of equipment that have rotating take-off and/or blades, but I was taught well how to operate and use these safely.

It was not always work. There was lots of space to run around and play. Only drawback was that the neighboring farms were a distance apart and there were few other children living nearby.

It was great when I began my elementary schooling. Waysidelog School was a single-room school with 18 students from ages 6 to 14. It gave me many playmates and a whole new social learning.

Yippee... we can make nice!

We pump pail after pail of water from the pump in front of the one room school where I spent my elementary school days from 1951 to 59. We crossed the road, opened dad's fence, and headed towards and the pools of ice. Wow! There was of ice everywhere! We fall on it, get soaked, crack ribs, break arms and legs, cut chins. Life is good.

It takes a day and night to make ice. Then we take our Flexible Flyers, Whammos, and my Silver Streak (formerly my brother's) which I inherited - never had enough money to afford a new sled - I still have the Silver Streak in my garage – I've dreamed of teaching how to use it safely =- to the son I do not have.

We were pretty good about taking turns and not being hoggish (Junior Bauer and Chanticleer Sinkula being the exceptions). The long hard slippery climb is rewarded with the rush of adrenaline and I am back down to the bottom in seconds. Sometimes we was a rut and we went off course... under (hopefully) the World War I triple barbed wire and into Erwin Sinkula's

8

plowing and we flew off the sled, I cut my chin the year we got the 1956 Belair Chevy. I got blood on the seat...

Anyway, we made BLT's early one August morning. My brother Robert, "Bozo" got the lettuce and tomatoes and I was to wash them and pick the lettuce over, while Mama fried bacon. Of course I washed, but didn't open the lettuce, as Mary wanted to fling tit cups (milk inflators) at the pigs. "Bozo" made a sandwich and gave it to her. She put it on the table and said, thanks, but I'll wait till the worm crawls out. A scant minute later a 2 inch angle worm wriggled out of her sandwich. All eyes in the room instantly focused on me. There was no place to hide.

Bozo raised holy hell... he is always angry... never treats me like a brother... sadly, in later life I've had to treat him like a son and save him financially time after time in the late 1980s through 2002. He'll never pay all the money back... worse he'll never appreciate all I did for him or miss me if I die first.

Waysidelog School

Chapter 2

My School Years

Reflections

I have found that Christmas, a time when families and friends get together, is when I often recall events of the past but if there is a particular month when these events took place then it must be November. It will always be my benchmark bittersweet month. There are many memories.

Strangely, my earliest "memory" came before I was born, obviously one I didn't share, but I can picture it so vividly. It took place on Armistice Day, November 11, 1931 at tiny St. John's Catholic Church of Krok, Wisconsin. Mildred Julia Haszel and Arthur Anton Hinesh married on an unseasonably warm sunny day. Four children came later with a special spiritual bond between their first and their fourth (Donald Arthur died… in my mind he became a saint but two short months into his earthly life… he was their fourth child and shared the same birth date, April 20th).

And there's November 1st, All Saints Day, a Catholic Feast day I have always celebrated. My brother Donald and Cousin Mary's birthday fall in

November too. More than anyone, Mary taught me to respect women. That was a long time ago. I've never forgotten that.

So much for a "sweet" memory, now comes a "bitter" one that was very much part of contemporary and local history included in my education. The S.S. Edmund Fitzgerald, a famous Great Lakes freighter carrying a full cargo, 26,000 tons of taconite iron ore pellets, left from Superior, Wisconsin, on the afternoon of November 9, 1975 headed for a steel mill near Detroit. The following day at 7.10 pm she suddenly sank in Lake Superior and all of her crew of 29 lost their lives.

The true cause of her sinking has never been established though there have been many books written about it. There was a near hurricane winter storm with 35 feet high waves. One theory is that the high waves of the storm swamped her cargo hatches causing topside damage and subsequent structural failure. Another is that she may have shoaled in a shallow part of Lake Superior.

Two watershed events of my life fell on the 8th of November. They changed the way I thought about life and created an empathy and sensitivity. The first happened in 1954. I was ten years old and in the 4th grade at my one room elementary school, Waysidelog School.

In April 1954 the Mexicans came as certainly as the apple and cherry blossoms on the trees whose fruit they would harvest in August through October. They were migrants. In their colorful 2 ton IH and GMC and Chevy vintage trucks, they wound their way up from Galveston and other places in Texas to the north, to Wisconsin, God's Country and us.

They came to plant, and to harvest lettuce, beans, pickles, cherries, potatoes, apples, peas, sugar beets. There was a migrant camp which was occupied only from April to November. It had a sugar beet elevator and was at the intersection of 29 W and C near Bob and Joanne Karl's farm.

I first met Arturo and Rosalinda Gonzales around my birthday (April 20). It was 1954. The family rented Vic Siebold's three-storey house along with two other migrant families. The kids were nearly chocolate brown and spoke broken English. Both wore crucifixes as would many Mexican (now they are called Hispanic) kids. They inspired such curiosity in me. Could Jesus have been chocolate brown?

As you know probably have gathered by now, I came from the breed of the "pitchfork farmer". Four months under the hot sun moving hay, oats, barley, wheat all by hand. Eight calluses on my small hands survive to this day. No Little League or Stars of Carlton - all my summers were working ones. Small wonder I later worked three jobs at once for years. There was no time then to be friends with the Gonzales kids, that was put on hold.

Rosalinda (Rosie) was even prettier when it came to September. I was now in my 5th grade. There was a new teacher. The wonderful Erna Teske replaced cranky Dorothy Kazimierczak. School was a joy again. Arturo was in 4th grade. Rosie in 3rd. I helped her with English lessons. I so looked forward to seeing her each day. Life was sweet.

And then, on the 8th of November, 1954 life changed forever. For all of us. A chimney fire, a three-storey house was consumed in minutes. All the money the Gonzales had was consumed in flames. They kept it in dollar bills in a shoebox. It was all their spring and summer earnings.

St. Joseph's and St. Peter's took collections, neighbors (including us) boarded the three families. One week later they headed for the South, and never returned. Before they left Rosie and I wept unashamedly in each other's arms and knew it would be the last time we would see each other.

I still have Betty's wagon...

Since Christmas 1952 a part of me has been in love continuously with Betty Sinkula (I don't know her married name). I was in the second grade and she in the eighth at Waysidelog "Busy Beaver' elementary school on Carlton Town Hall Road across from the former Hinesh Homestead. She was so beautiful and the fact that in my eight years of Xmas gift exchanges there, that year she drew my name, and her gift far surpassed any other... it was a genuine real rubber tired McCormick Deering grain wagon, an exact replica of the one we used on Ray Folks farm a decade later!

What was not to love then? Especially since the '51 gift from Arthur Tulacher was such a "clunk", a pre-opened and used puzzle (Girl with a duck, parts missing, I should add!)

I adored Betty the remainder of the year, and hence forth, and always will. She had Lucy's (her Mom's) angelic face and a great figure. Did that even register with a 7 1/2-year-old? It did!

Reality soon set in... I'd never school with her again... When I entered Kewaunee High School in September '59 she was two years departed. Oh, I'd look across the gravel road while working alfalfa and oats with my pitchfork and shocking barley ("shocking" involves picking up bundles of grain and stacking them up in high "teepees" so they can dry off before storing).

I had hoped to catch a glimpse of Betty in the vegetable garden... I did but stammered out "Hello", and "Nice day, eh?" and listened for a reply that seemed straight out of heaven. How I longed to grow up quick and marry her before Summer, else someone snatched her away forever.

When I shared that idea with Mama she reminded me that those plans "slightly" interfered with my Priesthood urges. Cousin Mary wasn't much more help when I disclosed my "crush", saying she had Betty pegged as my second cousin (I'm still unable to figure out that genealogy!). And, as such, I'd still go to hell with or without hot oil if I married Betty or her (my first cousin Mary). Problems, problems.

Several years later it was rumored that Betty had left home under dubious circumstances. She had become a young expectant mother... And was whisked away to a home for unwed mothers in Oregon, Wisconsin. I don't know ("MYOB") said Mama, and I did and to this day I still don't know what really happened... 'cept I never really fell out of love with her.

Oh she'd come back every few years in Summer for a visit and I'd seen her with Lucy at Sears (where the museum and submarine "Cobia" now are) in Manitowoc, or Janda's General Store (old Stangles) in Tisch Mills... the last time was '72. Fresh back from Vietnam and wearing the Beret, I found myself just as tongue-tied as that eight-year-old kid stammering across the gravel so many years ago. Some things never change...

I think she always knew and understood... And felt good about my admiration but it's always been and always will... like ships that pass in the night... You see dear reader, the old Bohemian Catholic way was "The man must be older!", by at least one day... or else... A big howl ensued when Henry Paska married Aunty Rose Hasszle... she two years his senior... dire predictions of doom notwithstanding, the marriage was in its 63rd year when uncle Hans passed. So much for doom...

How times have changed... Leo married Elaine 20 plus years his senior... a great match tempered with the realism that odds are against great marital longevity... but they both understood that going in, and it's been a great match...

The 1950 Baltimore Catechism also opposed marriages with over seven year age difference in males being older... How that magic number was obtained, God only knows, maybe something to do with Old Testament book of leave Leviticus which goes into some detail on seven years of prosperity, followed by seven years of plagues, curses, and whatnots... So with Daddy born in 12/02 and mama in 7/10 they missed the cut off by some seven months... Yet it wasn't all that bad a match was it? Daddy died two months short of their 49th anniversary, so it's not so much the age difference as it is the ages at the time of falling in love... If he is 30 and she is 16... Lookout trouble big-time!

If he is 60 and she is 46, what's the big howl about there? Especially in view of the fact that she is a much better judge of human character and political backstabbing than he is... It isn't the age, it's the intuitive judgment that counts there...

I'll have more to say about the Sinkula's in future chapters... about Frank ("the Dandy") Hinesh according Mayme, she the pupil... he the schoolteacher at Wayside... about their wonderful offspring Cousin Joanie scheming to marry off widow Grandma Mary Sinkula to Grandpa Frank Hinesh... She the "Dragon Lady"... he the Kaiser Wilhelm's long-lost stepbrother with tempers to match... Talk about the perfect setting for a double homicide! ever mix Nitro with C-4 ? Ya don't wanna, trust me!

I love the late Erwin and Lucy so... I'll always love Betty and wonder about what might have been. I have an annual photo of the Waysidelog school teacher and kids (population range 26 to 32) depending on the year. I'm uncertain which year it was. "Mikey" will always be my favorite...

Meanwhile she has seen it and can verify that I still have Betty's wagon and forever will.

Ages 8 to 14 Buck Night at the Lakeview: 1953

Wednesday night was buck nite: one dollar per car and no limit on people. We went to the Lakeview outdoor movie theater, maybe one to two times a month. Today only the sign remains on Memorial Drive just off from Mid-Cities Mall and just down from a.m. 980 WCUB. There were five of us and "The Kaiser" - (Grandpa – the only one save for Sainted Grandpa George Haszel who died before I was born). We saw such outstanding fare as "Seven Brides for Seven Brothers" and "Bear Country", (though the inevitable fog came and wiped out BC, and out of frustration everyone honked, due to the early ending. That was pretty much our recreation other than Christmas and church picnics (and our crabby old priest told us not to patronize the non-Catholic parishes).

Oh, yes, at the outdoor we got a burger or dog, popcorn and soda. I just don't remember French fries or brats from the early 1950s. Walking to/from the snack bar, I sometimes saw things I didn't understand: why for instance, during the middle of a perfectly good bear feature were people scrunched down in the backseat tightly arm locked and seemingly, on top of one another and making what was the light snoring or howling, or was it moaning sounds? Who in their right mind would want to miss the feature and snooze that time of night? I go back to the car after the snack bar, restroom routine and start describing what I saw and been start asking questions (remember I was eight or nine) Pa'd get very quiet, I think Mama blushed and Bozo told me to shut up and watch the Bears. So what was up with that? I turned the other cheek and cried.

The Green Bay Circus

"The Green Bay Circus", in the form of Carol and Mary Conrad (Elsie's girls), came to Hinesh farm for 2 - 3 weeks in late July. I got some education (no sex) from them and I really got to like and respect girls in my earliest years of noticing them. In fact I did most everything Mary wanted except put on lipstick and my sister's dress — would'a got killed for that.

Don't cross him!

Bob Sinkula was in grade 5, I in grade 7. He was a bigger kid... My height, strong for grade 5 and he had his grandpa Adolph Sinkula 's temper. Don't cross him! I found out the hard way. In the boys anteroom we got into a silly argument about which end of the baseball bat was the stock, and which was the barrel. We played a lot of imaginary war and we had to improvise with bats because no one had any toy rifles. Most of us were poor toys were a luxury.

The argument escalated and he turned away, only to wheel about and do a right hand hook into my right ear. It was a hard punch and I saw a few stars and went to my knees. No one else was there. He had run off. I started to cry... It hurt a lot... my ear rang for at least a day. Jimmy Staab heard me sobbing and came in to comfort me (by then it was well-known I had a crush on his sister, Patti). I felt so foolish, mumbling something about suing him... The pain ebbed but the ringing didn't. Minutes later Bob came back and apologized. Naturally I accepted and that was the end of it but I never went to his farm to play after that. And had lost my first fight. Be right... be brave, have faith. I wasn't that day. Lesson learned: never assault anyone... Fight only to defend and save myself. I've <u>never</u> violated that lesson.

My High School Years

1959 to 1963: Carol Lynn Belleau... she never knew... How much I cared.

I first saw her in "Rocky" Myers' Freshman Civics class on a sunny early September day. What joy! As seats were assigned, I got to sit across from her. Horn rimmed black pearl glasses, beautiful teeth, thin, an apple and peaches perfect face, pretty and neat and always clean... What was not to love in her? My first serious non-puppy love... she became the band major (twirler) leader... showed me a lot of moxie leading Frosh–Seniors in marching. I got in the front marching row directly behind her... <u>poetry in motion</u>... what a lovely tush !

How to say... "Hello and I love you"... tell me what is your name... Hello I love you and let me jump in your game! But not really. I never got the courage to talk to her that year till near the end when I sang Casey Jones: Ballad of the Train Wreck Engineer" to her as we mercifully got to share the back bus seat on a music trip. I blushed and my voice cracked. She loved the song and smiled sweetly at me. She was to sign my yearbook, "love". But was it already too late. A Sophomore fullback name "Jisa" already was developing an interest in her (he would later marry her.) I <u>never</u> told her how I cared. In April 1960, on Good Friday, I nearly tipped the Farmall "C" into the gully, thinking about her (I would have died but for my angel). I never told her, or proved my true love for her. Have I made the same mistakes now with the last, best love of my life?

On Stage

A sense of the dramatic was developed and a natural shyness and fear of being "on stage" had been overcome by practicing speeches to the chickens and the cats. I reckon this made me half-way good at it though my "audience" at the farm gave me mostly mixed reviews.

I took a four minute speech to the Regional Finals held in Oshkosh, Wisconsin and helped win the 1963 North-eastern Wisconsin Conference Championship Debate Trophy (actually my school tied with Green Bay Preble High School). The trophy is in a display case at Kewaunee High School and it has my name inscribed on it. It was sweet revenge over Mr. Delvaux. He had told me not to join the Debating Group, because me being in it for only one year would be a waste of his time and mine.

Mr. Miller's Senior English course and Mr. Rock Meyer's Social Problems course were my two favorites. Mr. Miller gave me unusual latitude. I was the vice president of my class, a gym rat who spent most of his leisure time playing sports or working out, and because of my literary and sports achievements I was awarded a special sweater with my school's insignia and initials and made a Letterman. I was also a West Point candidate. Mr. Miller told me that "Rock" and he were impressed by my achievements as a Senior high school student and that they both expected me to go far in life. Whatever I did.

So, in Miller's English IV class I knew I had a license to practice the unusual. We had a number of required oral presentations, so a ten-minute "your choice" play became NBC televison's Huntley-Binckley Evening News (my gal pal Mary Schultz became David Brinkley and I, Chet Huntley – this team was the number one Evening News in the late 50's and 60's).

We distorted it using the Smothers Brothers format. Mary was the totally straight one and me, well, I was completely goofy just like Tommy Smothers. Everyone loved it and I remember Miller's weird laugh. Looking back on it now he probably was thinking, "Let the good times roll at

20

Kewaunee High School" for it's their last days of innocence before they go into the working world and the true reality of life sets in.

The last presentation of the fall was a ten-minute drama presentation. Miller expected me to do something from Shakespeare. I gave them Hitler, Hood and Bismarck instead. My inspiration came from a copy of the "Sinking of the Bismarck" I bought in a bookstore just off Capitol Square in Madison, Wisconsin. That was in the Spring when I played "Lyric Interlude" on the trombone at the state finals and narrowly missed getting a gold medal.

I remember that "Mad Jack" Rider took a look at the large print style and promptly called me "retarded" to which I replied by dumping a glass of water down his pants.

Anyway, back to English IV drama presentation. None of my classmates knew exactly what to expect from me. I had a very dry sense of humor and a flair for doing the unusual. I threw everyone off track by asking to go 25th out of 25 (last), promising I'd be a tough act to follow. Guess so, especially since I was the last act.

The "D-Day" of English IV drama presentation came. The rules allowed us to read from a script. There were no stipulations about singing or other entertainment, but we had to keep it clean of course. I had organized my ten-minutes into half reading and half singing, plus or minus 15 seconds (within tolerance limits).

I had come a long way from delivering speeches to chickens and cats and by late 1962 I was confident when speaking or singing in front of large groups and had introduced several lyceum programs (open forums) to a more than 450 student body as well as doing a few basketball and football "pep rallies". So, I was ready and loaded to go.

21

I had prepared a handout for my audience. It was several pages extracted from Will L. Shirer's "The Sinking of the Bismarck". Shirer was a World War II correspondent and he describes how the German warship sank the British ship H.M.S. Hood. The loss of Britain's greatest warship was a disaster for the Allies. Immediately after its sinking Winston Churchhill ordered the Bismark must be destroyed. My presentation emphasized this rally call that the Bismark must be sunk.

I asked them to read through the text very slowly and deliberately, because I knew that many, especially, the ladies were new to the topic of naval battle. I knew the pages well and barely looked at the script and maintained a lot of eye contact with my classmates instead. Especially with Mary, Muzzi (Gary Mazanet who would later join the Marines) and my best buddy who had been nicknamed "Nude". He was called that before I met him at Kewaunee High School. He was Terry Neumeier who would die a Marine three short years later. I was prepared for giving the speech of my life.

I overdid it. It's like I'd transposed myself on the foredeck of H.M.S. (His Majesty's Steamship) Battleship Hood (Was it named after Robin Hood? No, I found out it was named after British Admiral Samuel Hood). For a split second, I saw the 15 inch shell hit the ship between centre and stern, explode the ammunition in the magazines, and blow the ship in half sending all but three sailors to their death. There were 1,416 crew who lost their lives and only three survivors. Ted Briggs, William Dundas and Bob Tilburn were rescued from the freezing waters (I saw Ted Briggs on the History Channel in 2008 shortly before he died).

After I said the sentence "The Hood had blown up" I bowed my head in silent prayer for 30 seconds, but where had the lump in my throat come from? Why did I emit quiet sobs and my eyes produce tears? That was not in the script! I had not planned on this. Why in my mind's eye did I also see the dive bombing of a Japanese navy "Kate" bomber aircraft releasing the 1,760 lb armor piercing bomb down the U.S.S. Arizona's stack at Pearl Harbor? The magnitude of the result was similar with 1,177 of the 1,400 crew losing their life.

And why was there the image of the heavy cruiser U.S.S. Indianapolis (CA-35) being torpedoed by an Imperial Japanese Navy I-58 submarine? (The United States Navy did not know of the sinking until four days later when survivors were found by a routine patrol ship. There were 1,196 crewmen aboard and approximately 300 went down with the ship. From the remaining crew of 880 who had too few lifeboats and little or no food and drinking water, and were subject to shark attacks, there were only 316 survivors.)

It took but a few seconds for this unholy trinity of naval disasters to flash across my private mental stage. For the only time in high school my 24 cherished classmates saw me openly weep and witnessed my tenderness, humanity and humility.

I had to regain control of myself. I looked over at "Nude", his face was gray and his eyes were also in tears. I'd see that same flesh tone of his next in his coffin three years later. Was it that "Nude" and I in 1962 sub-consciously knew or had some premonition that one of us would not survive what lay ahead? The girls were all weeping. The guys were clearing throats with heads down. Come on Mark!

"Dear class, the late great Johnny Horton, so tragically lost in an auto wreck three years ago, forever immortalized this epic battle. May I please now sing for you the rest of this chilling but true footnote to history when *Duty, Honor and Country* carried the Free World to survival."

23

With that said I poured my heart and soul into the song "Sink the Bismarck". There was no piano or accompaniment and it was not needed. Seriously, I don't think I've ever sang anything better. Excerpts from the lyrics are reproduced here:

In May of 1941 the war had just begun
The Germans had the biggest ship that had the biggest guns
The Bismarck was the fastest ship that ever sailed the sea
On her decks were guns as big as steers and shells as big as trees...

The Hood found the Bismarck and on that fatal day
The Bismarck started firing fifteen miles away
We gotta sink the Bismarck was the battle sound
But when the smoke had cleared away the mighty Hood went down
For six long days and weary nights they tried to find her trail
Churchill told the people put every ship asail
Cause somewhere on that ocean I know she's gotta be
We gotta sink the Bismarck to the bottom of the sea
We'll find the German battleship...

The fog was gone the seventh day and they saw the morning sun
Ten hours away from homeland the Bismarck made its run
The Admiral of the British fleet said turn those bows around
We found that German battleship and we're gonna cut her down...

We had to sink the Bismarck cause the world depends on us
We hit the deck a runnin' and we spun those guns around
Yeah we found the mighty Bismarck and then we cut her down
We found the German battleship...

[Johnny Horton recorded this song *Sink The Bismarck* in 1960 (it may have been inspired by Shirer's book or the 1960 British war movie of the same name). The song was written by Tillman Franks and Johnny Horton. It made the Top Ten in both the Country and Pop charts.]

I totally lived that song that day. As was the custom in the class, I did not expect any applause and I did not receive any.

It was a gray and rainy day, we were nearing the end of our High School years and I sensed that many of us were experiencing our private epiphanies of life, of death, what the future would hold for us, and of infinity. By October 1962 twenty-five of our class were 18 years old and had come of age. We were adults.

The Cuban missile confrontation was unresolved until October 28, 1962, when President John F. Kennedy and the United Nations Secretary - General U-Thant made secret agreements and public ones with Khrushchev. Would these agreements end the fear there was going to be a nuclear war? We were in an era when it was impossible to comprehend the reality that lay ahead.

The dismissal bell rang. Several of the girls hugged me on the way out. Guys clapped me on the shoulder. A speechless "Nude" walked with me to the bus (bus #10) in the rain.

A Major Life Decision

My most important "fork in the road decision" was made on the terrible date of August 30th, 1965 when "Nude" my high school buddy, Marine Lance Corporal Terry J. Neumeier was killed in action at DaNang, South Vietnam. Farming for me would forever be left behind. I devoted all my energy to finish at the head of my Army Reserve Officers' Training Corps (R.O.T.C) and volunteered for the war effort in Vietnam.

Another 80-acre farmer bought my parents' farm the following year as I entered Basic Training. After five generations (1874-1966) the Hinesh Family left farming behind, something I'll always deeply regret. In 1967, I graduated from the R.O.T.C. and business administration programs at St. Norbert College in West De Pere, Wisconsin.

Living in a community where Christmas is very much celebrated, I think it has something to do with why many of my "ghosts" and recollections of the past often appear then. It's a special religious holiday when families get together and we get in touch with friends.

Chapter 3

Vietnam 1969 to 1971

My time in Vietnam was from January 1969 until October 1971. I was an officer. My first assignment was in the Tank Brigade of the 5th Mechanized Infantry Division until November 1969. Then I served as a Captain with Army Special Forces in Vietnam and Cambodia from December 1969 to October 1971. During my third continuous tour of duty I was airlifted and medevaced back to the United States.

[For those unfamiliar with the term "medevace" it means "to transport a person by air (usually by helicopter) to a place where they can receive medical care".]

The military awards I received were four Bronze Stars, the Army Commendation Award, and Vietnamese Special Forces Parachute Wings, and the Cross of Gallantry.

Remember, the 8th of November

When I was at St. Norbert College I read in the "Army Times" that a rifle platoon of thirty "Flying Winged Swords" of the 173rd Airborne Brigade were set upon by Viet Cong soldiers in wooded terrain. They had little air support and only five survived. It happened on the 8th of November, 1965. The same month and day the Gonzales family's house went on fire (that was in 1954).

After Marine Terry Neumeier, my classmate was killed, and then Dan, another classmate shortly afterwards, I went to the R.O.T.C. Commandants office to formally volunteer for Vietnam and the 173rd Flying Winged Swords. Colonel Babler told me I must wait. Less than two years later I flew to the Pentagon to have my request fulfilled. This time I was honored and the 173rd would be mine to serve.

And, why not? I was in a class of thirty-two lieutenants in the St. Norbert College, R.O.T.C. and was first in my R.O.T.C. class-work. The pain of not having been accepted for West Point was no longer there.

On January 31, 1968 during the TET holiday which is celebrated in Vietnamese Society for several days as a time to visit family and friends, the North Vietnamese Army (NVA) and the Viet Cong (VC) made massive and coordinated attacks through out South Vietnam. This nasty campaign, the NVA/VC TET Offensive, brought changes in military strategies (see Notes for TET Offensive).

When I arrived in Vietnam in January 1969 I was diverted to a heavy tank brigade of the 5th Mechanized Infantry Division at DongHa, DMZ (see Notes). That was where I was most needed. It was clear that I would not be a Flying Winged Sword in the 173rd.

Vietnam, July, 1969

July is the hottest, driest month of the year and has the clearest nights. The Southern Cross gleams down, desperately trying to impart a measure of peace and goodwill amidst chaos, madness and death.

The Tank Brigade of the 5th Mechanized Infantry Division was known as the "Red Devils" of the DMZ. Out-manned and out-gunned maybe 10 to 1 if we were lucky. We had tanks, big artillery guns, and our gunships controlling the air, but "they", the Viet Cong/North Vietnamese Army had the numbers and they were native and knew the terrain far better than we did. They had the advantage.

I had begun my active duty in Vietnam in January 1969 and was now into my sixth month in DongHa. By day I ran a Personnel Action Shop, a training platoon to orient newcomers to the many dangers which lay ahead of them. By training I was a Civil Affairs Personnel Officer but in reality I was a dog-faced rifle soldier, trying to see one more day for mine and me.

Each fifth night I commanded "Sector Tiger", the north-east quadrant that butted up against the heavy jungle. (It was four months later, in October 1969 that a tank of the 3rd Marine Division would save us and give me a measure of valour under attack.) Every fifth night I was on duty from 1800 hrs (6 pm) to 0600 hrs (6 am). I commanded 30 fortified bunkers and gun emplacements, and several hundred meters of concertina wire, fougasse (high explosive napalm) trip flares, anti-personnel mines, noise makers to detect "them", to keep "them" out...to keep "us" in... and alive.

My quadrant of the four was the most probed and most heavily attacked over a two year span. That warm July night ...0200 hours... was it the 8th or 9th of July? ...a detail that does not matter. I was on guard duty and walking midway between Bunker 6 and Bunker "Lucky 7". I froze and all the hairs on my body stood up and I could not breathe or swallow. I sensed death and I was paralysed with fright.

A microsecond later, the jungle night quiet was broken by a hellish roar. In the light of a three quarter moon I saw it leap over the trip flares and concertina wires in one long single bound. It was an Asian tiger that weighed three or four hundred pounds. I had frozen in place. If I'd taken three more paces it would have knocked me over and what would have become of me then? In the moon light I saw one large eye and it did look satanic. In an instant it turned around and went back the same way it had come. The adjacent Northwest Sector was called "Leopard". This was a tiger from Sector Leopard that had attempted to get into Sector Tiger. (There are leopards found in the wild in Vietnam, but they weigh around 30 pounds and are very much smaller than the Asian tiger.)

I did not become a meal that night. A group of tigers or a single man-eating tiger had killed two marines from the 3rd Marine Division. I could easily have been the third if it had not been for my sense of danger. It is one memory I shall never forget. Sometimes I awake from a dream during the night, startled, feeling fear and remembering this incident.

Rest and Recreation

The week after I left in November 1969 to go to Saigon for a week of administrative functions and rest, a sapper attack succeeded. Both Francisco Fuentes and Reynaldo Quenos died from LAWS (lite anti-tank weapons) along with most of the personnel who were in the two bunkers. They were the "Mad Mex" and "Pineapple Boy". Rey's family farmed sugar cane and pineapples in Puerto Rico and they told me they were known as the "black sheep" brothers. They did everything together.

I remember when I went on recreation leave with them to Hong Kong to buy $600 of stereo equipment. Officers were allowed $100 more than others. The "black sheep brothers" came along and each spent their $500 allowance on prostitutes. They had a lot of fun. I bought the stereo system I wanted but I ended up storing it in a closet because I was unable to use it until I found larger housing.

Francisco and Reynaldo died. Had I remained on duty in Sector Tiger after November 11th, 1969, I would have been dead too. I did not know they had died until mid-September 1991 when I read their names on the wall of the Vietnam memorial in Washington, D.C.

On guard duty in my headquarters (it was a bunker), I sometimes preached "Jesus" to "my boys" and warned them not to go with loose women. They'd laugh and say "Lieutenant we love ya, you're a great guy but you're so full of shit". It was a lost cause.

A "replacement policy" was used in Vietnam. It this context the term has a different meaning than replacing American forces with South Vietnamese forces. What it meant for me was that an entire unit would be used to replace another to sustain the role of a unit in battle. It was a "systems approach" to battle. Further casualties within a unit were replaced by individual soldiers. That raised issues about the fitness of a soldier within a unit if he had not had collective training with others in his unit. Due to the scale of the Vietnam war and the high number of casualties there was a frequent movement of soldiers. Comrades were constantly having to connect with new people.

Friendly Fire

We did landline cimmo (telephone) checks complete with passwords. I'd walk the sector once or twice an hour depending on perceived enemy activity, using passwords and check each bunker. SP4 Timothy Wold from Thief River Falls, Minnesota, newly arrived "in country" had panicked, forgotten the password, and was in near total darkness and unable to see who I was. He jammed the barrel of his M-16 into my solar plexus. He came very close to pulling the trigger.

And once James Holden Stadt from Iowa City (he was called the "secret squirrel") came very close to shooting me. He was a sergeant and ran the communications shack (a number one enemy target priority). He controlled all classified documents to Top Secret level. He tripped in the dark and simultaneously fired his gun. I felt the "hot breath" of a dozen M-16 rounds zip past my left ear.

Those two incidents made the danger of "friendly fire", very clear to me "friendly fire", especially when with soldiers who are inexperienced and who may panic. It is not something that happens only when engaged in an attack and anonymously mistaking one's own or other friendly forces for enemy forces.

November 8th, 1969.

The replacement of me from my unit of the Tank Brigade of the 5th Mechanized Infantry Division came after I was given my 1st Bronze Star for calling in the Marine anti-aircraft tank to thwart a sapper attack designed to destroy Base Camp Red Devil. On the brink of battle fatigue, I was sent to Saigon for a week of administrative functions and rest.

The "spook" (CIA) part of me ferreted out the information that "Mad Jack" Wheeler, a mentor at Civil Affairs School, Indianapolis, years prior, had decided to move me to Special Forces. It was the beginning of my personal rebuilding program. I named it "Hoi Chan" – Open Arms. Now, I was member of the Special Forces. It was a great honor to be called to serve in them.

Indo-China Christmas 1969: When a Higher Power watched over me with good intentions.

Christmas 1969 was my first Christmas spent away from my home in Wisconsin. With the first of nearly three years in Vietnam-Cambodia at an end, I was finally doing what I liked best.

I had been transferred to the 5th Special Forces Group (Airborne), popularly known as the Green Berets, and my move had given me a new role. I was a Civil Affairs Officer and working face to face with native Vietnamese, Cambodes, Hmong, Montegnard, and other highland tribes. After Typhoon Dora had devastated Base Red Devil, Civil Affairs efforts were diminished and most Vietnamese and hill folks were pretty much ignored by the United States military.

I was assigned to run Civil Affairs. This was my element. After having spent my first eight months with a tank brigade, it was a very different challenge with new dangers but it was refreshing for me to have been given it.

Several native schools and orphanages existed in the local countryside and I tried to help them all. They needed so much. "Uncle Ho" had died earlier that year. Late 1969 was so much better than early 1968 when the

TET offensive had wreaked havoc. In fact, it looked good for a Christmas cease-fire. So, I decided to outfit my areas schools and orphanages.

On December 24, 1969 I led a hodge-podge assortment of Lambretta scooters, Citroen 3-wheeled cars, Peugeot cars and various other ramshackle vehicles. We headed out to a U. S. Supply/Refuse Holding Area (essentially it was a "dump"). The route that morning had not been patrolled for mines or potential ambushes so it was a calculated risk and we ventured forth on faith.

Arriving at the depot, we overloaded everything that could haul anything. We hauled loads of military cast offs, desks, wall lockers, footlockers, chairs, usable clothes and just about anything that was not nailed or tied down or too badly damaged or weather beaten. All of it was needed.

With the loading nearly concluded as the day was ending, I was in a real feel-good mood and wandered over to a group of salvageable armoured vehicles.... damaged jeeps, an M-48 Patton tank which had evidently hit a vehicle mine, plus an array of 2 and a half ton trucks. But it was that APC (Armored Personnel Carrier) that caught my eye. Likely holed by RPG's (rocket propelled grenades) or LAWS (light anti-tank weapons) in an ambush, it would have been a death-trap for most or all of its crew who would have had little protection from the penetrating rounds of fire during the attack. I was mesmerized at seeing it and could only wonder about how many of my fellow soldiers had been killed in it. The feel-good emotion I had was replaced by feelings of despair about what war does. What was the cost of this? What human treasures would be sacrificed before there was an end to this war?

We needed to return home before dark. During the drive back, Hugo Montenegro's soundtrack of The Good, the Bad and the Ugly ran through my mind. I felt I had seen it all that day, and been forever changed. Perhaps it is best we cannot see or foretell the future.

Mercifully, I had no forecast of that eventual disaster, as we returned safely home and rejoiced in the thanks and tears of the orphans and nuns, that long ago and far away feel-good Christmas Eve in Vietnam in 1969.

November 1970

One year later, November 1970, I was running a small first-aid M.A.S.H type hospital (one doctor and native nurses - no American women were allowed that deep in the field) at Ban Me Thuot, plus rebuilding hamlets there as well. Those who required surgery or had other serious injuries were taken to by helicopter to Saigon for treatment.

It wasn't part of my medical and civil affairs duties but about the 12th of November (the days blur one into another when in harm's way), I left on a 16 day "tunnel rat" mission. I was in better shape than Craig, had a cool head and could prevent our Montegnards, Cao Dai, Himing, Cambodes and Chinese from killing each other. My best strength in Vietnam was that the natives all liked, respected or loved me. They saved my life more than once.

Sometime during the second week of this mission, we met with the 325th North Vietnamese Engineering Brigade who were rebuilding the Ho Chi Minh Trail. A similar fate to that of the 173rd platoon on November 11th, 1965 was now to be ours. All the stars and planets lined up. The whistles and bells of my ESP went off. Pol Vang, our Cambodian scout, sniffed out that soldiers of the NVA were nearby, just out of effective killing fire range. CPT Craig gave his famous "run" command. Vang and I at the very front laid down covering AK-47 fire when the NVA soldiers discovered we were retreating. We opened fire. I expanded my last magazine into them to delay their advance.

CPT Craig recommended me for the Silver Star. I got my 4th Bronze instead.

Chapter 4

My Heartland

It was important to include this chapter. My aim was to write a book that was near complete in itself. It provides a history that I hope shall be useful to put in context details about Wisconsin that appear in other chapters.

The Making of My Wisconsin

In the early 1800's, the "Wisconsin Territory", as designated on Federal maps, extended south from Copper Harbor to present day Chicago suburbs and east from the Mississippi River to the west shore of Lake Michigan. When Illinois achieved statehood in 1818, territorial land from south of Lake Geneva to Chicago was ceded to the "Land of Lincoln". Nineteen years later Michigan's statehood gained the entire Upper Peninsula from Wisconsin Territory.

A decade later in 1848, our 30th State was established with its present boundaries...a true "God's Country" of over 15,300 lakes, thousands of pristine rivers, virgin timberlands, and mineable resources.

The trappers, miners, and Native Americans were from Europe who sought a new world, leaving behind wars, pestilences, and famines. Because water travel was preferred and much easier than overland (which obviously lacked roads and bridges way back then), a very popular access to our new state was upriver on the Mississippi from the port of New Orleans. This was the route which my Great-Great-Grandparents and thousands of Bohemians followed.

An article I had published in "Badger History" while a 7th grader at Waysidelog School, Town of Carlton, Kewaunee County, based on a 1957 interview with my Grandfather, Frank J. Hinesh describes this marvelous adventure in quest of a new farming life.

The immigrants of the 1830's -1870's took flatboats up the "Father of Waters". Since the Mississippi flowed from North to South, from Minnesota to the Gulf of Mexico, is meant that moving upstream necessitated very hard work for the rowers and oarsmen, and the new Americans all had to take there turns helping with this to defray the passage fare and reach their destinations.

A major "fork in the road" decision was taken at the convergence of the Mississippi and Wisconsin Rivers. To some degree, ethnic and ancestral heritage dictated which "fork" was chosen.... namely the South Europeans (i.e. Slaves, Serbs), East Europeans (Bohemians, Polish), Belgians, and Dutch tended to take the Wisconsin flowage and settle in Northeastern Wisconsin especially in Brown, Door, Kewaunee, Manitowoc, and Outagamie counties and have remained there 4-5 generations to the present point in time.

On the other hand, the North Europeans and Scandinavians generally stayed the course of the Mississippi Northward and settled in Wisconsin's St. Croix Valley and Minnesota's Red River Valley. The Germans and West Europeans tended to go to either location and are quite equally divided between both Wisconsin and Minnesota.

Depending on their means, the new Wisconsin settlers purchased anywhere from 20 to 120 acre parcels. Mining copper, iron ore, and other minerals was ending due to resource depletion. "Slash lumbering" (widespread cutting and burning without replanting) and the massive Peshtigo fire ended Wisconsin's role as the main timber producer of the early 1800's. Land was cleared for planting vegetables, grains, and legumes and other hay crops to feed animals. At one point in the 1800's, Wisconsin was "America's Breadbasket" with its wheat, oat and barley crops, a significant amount of which was used in malting of fermented beverages, especially beer. The plains states such as Kansas soon overtook Wisconsin in wheat production. Post-Civil War years then saw Wisconsin become America's #1 corn producer. But soon Iowa and Nebraska surpassed us due to deeper and richer top-soils more suited to providing nitrogen and other elements which corn depleted from croplands.

Having been used to raising cattle, swine, and poultry in their Old Country, our new settlers shifted Wisconsin's agricultural base to animal production, especially dairy farming as the 1800's wound down. They raised produce and animals and milk for their own needs and bartered or sold the excess. Gradually the small farms expanded, especially in acreage and dairy herd size. 40 acres became 60, thence 80. Eighty acres became 120, thence 160. The seeds of today's corporate and mega-farms with hundreds and thousands of milking stock were sewn in the combination and expansion of the 40 and 80 acre plots our families bought so many years ago in the mid 1800's.

Cheese factories sprung up rapidly, about 1 per 4 square miles. Dairy agriculture thrived and grew, resulting in the Wisconsin Milk Marketing Board getting "America's Dairyland" added to Wisconsin license plates in 1939 where it remains to this present day. While it's true that California has surpassed us in total milk cows and milk tonnage, we need not fear the loss of that esteemed title for the following historical reasons:

1. Most importantly, in all milk, cheese, and other dairy national and international competitions, Wisconsin products tend to win the "lions share" of the awards.

Experience, craftsmanship, and dedicated hard work result in this.

2. Wisconsin's first state fair held in Janesville in 1851 emphasized agricultural dairy commodities at a time when California was still in its "gold rush," so Wisconsin effectively had a near century head start in the dairy industry. In 1872 we started a Board of Trade for marketing Wisconsin cheese, followed by State cheese makers creating Colby and Brick cheese in 1874 and 1875.

3. Dairy science has always been Wisconsin's strong suit. University of Wisconsin's College of Agriculture offered Educational Degrees in the 1880's and established the first Dairy School in the U.S. in 1891. This was one year after Stephen Babcock, an agricultural chemist at the University of Wisconsin, developed the Babcock test to determine milk richness and butterfat content which is still in present use. 1895 saw Wisconsin introduce the first commercial pasteurizing machine for milk quality and safety, plus good taste!

4. By 1900 Wisconsin surpassed all other states in cheese and dairy production. Soon a cheese grading program, tied to a licensed cheese maker program was started. By 1922, Wisconsin cows reached 2.36 million head. A Wisconsin Milk Marketing Board was established, followed by the Wisconsin National Dairy Promotion and Research Board. The University of Wisconsin Madison Center for Dairy Research, and the Wisconsin Specialty Cheese Institute added quality and marketability worldwide to Wisconsin's specialty cheese industry. Wisconsin assumed national leadership in cheese volume and variety, offering more than 360 varieties, types, and styles of cheese made under the supervision of Wisconsin licensed cheese makers. Given all these facts and 150 years of historical achievements, a reasonable person would likely conclude that "American's Dairyland" is in the best hands and rightfully should remain on the license plates of our 30th and "Forward" State.

Recent trends have seen the average size of Wisconsin dairy herds on the rise. By 2007, more than 6,000 Wisconsin farms had a minimum of 50 milking cows. Therein lies the challenge ... given excessive inflation in energy, fertilizer and seed grain costs, it's almost imperative that to remain competitive and earn a decent living, quality must be maintained and farm capacity be increased. Farms need to enlarge in order to remain competitive and financially viable, and this situation affects virtually all our 17,000 dairy operations today, whether they milk 10 or 1000 cattle.

Actually, this challenge was already noticeable in the 1940's and 1950's. Modernization and expansion was necessary back then when buildings, machinery, and land weren't so inflation prone. Farmers such as Leonard Sinkula did just that and provided a wonderful legacy to their children and grand children in that those who wanted farming careers have all been successful and century farms have resulted. My own Grandfather lacked such vision, and beyond us purchasing a Farmall M with a 'Little Genius' two bottom plow for $1,100 in 1945 and a Farmall 200 with mower and cultivator for $1,900 in 1956, we didn't really move forward beyond a 22 cow milkherd. Thus, as we grew up, my sister Marie, my brother Robert, and I realized there would have to be careers other than farming for us.

I saw huge changes in the `50's and `60's:

1. Cattle stopped being moved from pasture to pasture and were fed in feedlots from green chopper bulk feed wagons and silo haulage from conveyors. This greatly cut down on waste that pasturing caused. There was more fertile land now available to be farmed with crops.

2. Artificial insemination opened a vast new area of genetic breeding, enhancing production, butterfat content, and stronger, longer lifespan cattle. This brought another upside with the elimination of dangerous breeding bulls who could would charge at you and wreak havoc upon people as I found out on two occasions as a youngster. Fortunately I was good runner and fast enough to escape.

3. Widespread use of fertilizers. The fertilizer spreader became as common as hay balers to supplement natural manure to greatly increase production. "Bloat - Guard" was used in green-lot feeding to prevent

asphyxiation in cattle from overeating and gasification in their stomachs causing death. We had lost our number one milk producing cow overnight, in three inch crop pasture, due to overeating. Also chemicals could be added to chopped hay to prevent spontaneous combustion resulting devastating hay barn fires.

4. Milk handling radically changed. From milk pail to milk can, to milk pail to cooling tank, farmers installed bulk tanks. Thus the milk can trucks disappeared as bulk tank trucks came upon the scene. Pipeline and milking parlors evolved, the milk can disappeared from the scene altogether.

5. Crop rotation, strip cropping, contour plowing, and waterway erosion control greatly improved crop yields, and showed we'd finally learned our lessons from topsoil erosion and the Dust Bowl effects of the 30's. For, once gone, precious topsoil can never be replaced.

These five changes mostly improved dairy agriculture, and farms that couldn't adapt to them (like my family) were absorbed by other larger operations. We truly had come a long way from the 1600's when dairy cows first reached the American colonies. In 1841 when Anne Pickett established Wisconsin's first "cheese factory" when she combined milk from her cows with milk from her neighbors cows and made it into cheese!

Wisconsin has seen much turbulence, as has my life. The wonderful State industries of J.I. Case (Racine), Allis Chalmers (Milwaukee), American Motors Rambler (Kenosha), and countless firms like Mirro of Manitowoc County have faded into history. NAFTA and other free trade agreements have contributed to this. GM at Janesville has closed. This State has an uncertain future. At one time it was second in the U.S. in industrial/manufacturing job employment. Too many industrial firms have left for cheaper labor and tax markets or have simply faded away.

We loyal "Badgers" still call this "God's Country." The badger is our state animal. Wisconsin became the "the badger state" way back in the 1800s because miners dug tunnels into hillsides searching for lead and then lived in them during the winter months to keep warm. This reminded people of badgers and Wisconsin became known as the badger state.

Our 1998 State Sesquicentennial stamp features a dairy farm, our 2004 Federal Quarter has the Holstein, the ear of corn, and the wheel of cheese. For, you see, having once traveled the world, I found that "the grass isn't greener on the other side." We still choose to live here, even when the tax situation isn't the best, or the winters either. For Wisconsin still is and shall always be "America's Dairyland" and, in the end, "There's no place like home."

Load of hay (early 1940's)

Chapter 5

Coming Home to Civilian Life

After Vietnam I had three civilian work careers. Returning to civilian life and adjusting after being a soldier was not easy. It took a while. I went 13 months before a career opportunity arose. I baled hay and tilled fields for $1.00 per hour just to keep busy. I applied for many jobs but my college degree from St. Norbert and my war record as a Captain in the Army Special Forces seemed to count for nothing to the paper mills, utility companies, manufacturers and other businesses. It was a familiar story for many who had returned from serving in Vietnam and were trying to find work and begin careers.

First I worked for the United States Government Social Security Administration. Next, I worked for the U.S. Army and Reserves. Then, I worked for the Kewaunee County Sheriff's Department. I obtained an Associate Degree of Police Science from Northeast Wisconsin Technical College (NWTC) and served five sheriffs with one term as Kewaunee County Undersheriff.

Serving my Community

Vietnam's positive legacy for me was to become a "caregiver." I have continued on from the farm and village programs with crop production enhancement, to water purification, to water buffalo inoculation in Civil Affairs Programs. I ran a Special Forces M.A.S.H. Hospital on the Cambodian frontier. I succeeded in making the adjustment to civilian life and enjoyed a successful career working for the Kewaunee Sheriff's Department. Over the past forty years I've increasingly given much of my spare time to better the lives of family, friends, and others materially, emotionally, and compassionately. Without the Vietnam experience, it's not certain that I'd have become a "caregiver" or doing volunteer work. I had left the farm to go to Vietnam, but kept the farmer within me.

Returning to Civilian Life and My First Job

After Vietnam, adjusting to civilian life presented a new challenge. In my first job, following the routine of office life with the main part of it being paperwork (it often seemed so trivial) and having an excess of it to do was difficult. Having to take instructions and orders from others for who I had little respect was also very difficult. This apparently is an issue that many face after leaving the military and begin civilian work. I bit the bullet and did my best to do my work correctly and efficiently.

In the office where I worked there were too many tensions. Much of that was based on my immediate boss — a married man with children - having an affair with a much younger female member of the staff. She received a promotion and whether it was true or not, most believed it had been given to her because of their social intimacy rather than on her work performance. Several of us believed that we had been passed over for

48

promotion. It is not an uncommon scenario and sometimes an "office affair" is harmless or merely rumor, but in this instance it was very obvious. Needless to say, I was pleased to put that job behind me and move on.

My next employment was with the U.S. Army and Reserves. Much of the time I was sitting at a desk and attending to paperwork but in this job I was much happier. I was assisting soldiers, many who had seen active Vietnam duty in Vietnam.

Requiem for a lost child

When I worked in the Kewaunee Sheriff's Department there were many times I encountered tragic events. It hit me hard to see a member of my community lose their life in tragic circumstances. The death of a child brings a very painful grief. It is the loss of a life that has been unfulfilled.

A week has passed since 16 year old Adam crashed into the waters of the Kewaunee River downhill from the seed farm. I understand that death was near instantaneous with very little pain being experienced. Two days later, I heard the stories of "too much speed", "he was talking on the phone", "eating in the car" and on and on about reasons why he was distracted. Knowing that there's a frequently used clear crossing at the hill's lower slope, I'd like to think that Adam had swerved to avoid hitting another vehicle and thus lost control; setting off the terrible chain of events. He's still in the water and needs to be brought home, soon, NOW!

Adam was a very normal 16 year old with hopes and dreams like his contemporaries in the Kewaunee High School student body. He always called his folks to tell them where he was. The Fourth commandment (Honor your Father and Mother) evidently meant something to him. I have no doubt he would have cared for his parents in their declining years, just as

49

I did for Daddy (for 10 years) and Mama (for 30 years); he just had it in him to be that way. And oh! He had the usual growing pains and gave his folks a hard time on occasion, but who of us, former teens, have not on some occasion? We all live in "glass houses, so don't throw stones, please!" Adam was maturing normally towards adulthood.

I can't feel the same pain that his parent's Gary and Mary feel about the loss of their son. They can't feel mine, the way I feel about the loss of Donald Arthur Hinesh (born 4/20/34 – died 6/6/34 from infantile pneumonia). The brother I never knew but can visualize and see in the arms of Frances Hinesh (Grandma who died in 1930).

I can empathize and provide understanding, support and love. "Lest We Forget"; one of my favorite sayings about my lost wartime comrades, Neumeier and Rogalski and the many others who lost their lives. I shall never ever forget.

In requiem, I rationalize that it's not how long you live, it's how well you live. My mother's words echo. Do no harm towards others, love one another, be right, be brave, and have faith. Sometimes I fail but I always try to follow these watchwords. Live life well for as long as God wills.

Our community will always have its legacy of memories of Adam who we knew as "Feddy". When we move forward we shall forever take his legacy forward with us.

The Remains of the Day

On St. Patrick's Day, 2006 I did wear green (it was the green shirt number 30 of the Green Bay Packers running back, Ahman Green. I celebrated by visiting at the rest home where my mother was. Mama's had been eating poorly and had lost 12 pounds in the last two weeks.

I remembered '88 when I took a date to the Karsten and we had all we wanted, making the Milwaukee Street Hill in her Jeep Cherokee (I didn't have a 4 x 4 those days). There was something like 17 inches of snow that St. Patrick's Day and Crandon Lumber saw fit to bring a horse to haul timber from a cedar swamp when the John Deere Skid Steer bogged down in the drifts pulling out logs.

Bittersweet memories! Ruth's love story at Perkins... Orville's Love story in Superior nearly 20 years back... is there a love story for me? I ache when I consider the terrible turmoil I've brought to her life... I know the unrest, worry, maybe even hurt I'm causing... what to do? The last page of a later chapter reveals it at all.

I'll love her, only Her, forever and a day... My last conscious thought will be of "Her" alone... "She" allows me into her life I'll spend the rest of mine bringing her great love, peace, joy, and security. I've bared my soul to her. Whatever changes I'll make in my life will be only those which make her happy... She knows she can make me over if she wishes... that she'll always have her way with me so while I'm asking so much of her, I'm also offering so much to Her and Her alone. The ninth Commandment notwithstanding, only God can take me away from her; only she can send me away from her.

Yesterday: that terrible crash on I 43/310. The cop telling me to alert the radio media 6 1/2 miles down the road. The living on the edge and 80 plus MPH to make that 12 PM news headline. The lady dies. Oh dear God why? Couldn't you have held back time for a mini-second to thus avert the crash?

Then the frantic trip down AB with 4 miles to cover in 3 min. to get her some of those wonderful weiners and sultz for Dad. And Brenda's laughing at me and calling me cheap because I had by accurate count, $10.47 on me. "I'm not so very impressed with you, Mark" said she trying to keep a straight face. But, I said I thought the meat was free to those wearing "green"! Laughter.

A Lost Love: Near you St. Patty's day 2006

A special day sadly marred by my having to assist at a multiple vehicle disaster. But earlier in the magical day... a story about "Forever".

The "Sorority of Four" came and sat next to me at the WCUB Radio Program at Perkins this a.m. I got the booth with microphone access as Lee Davis often solicits my "on-air" comments and I sometimes interview guests on air or off air as the situation warrants. With Dr. Kevin Kumpbale being interviewed at the table next to me, I still heard conversations of the four:

Ruth with white hair, was clearly the oldest and neatest in appearance. She evidently was an assistant librarian, single, and getting on in age when she met Ernie who was produce manager at Uncle Ray's ABC Supermarket on West Washington, Manitowoc so many years ago.

Her beautiful eyes, moist and luminous, shined while she talked of falling in love with an unhappily married man, their joint decision not to date or have an affair, and her promise to him to wait however long it would take. Oh the heartache she felt in the lengthy span of time it took before Ernie's wife chased and ran off and a legal divorce ensued... but finally, some years later, they became a couple, too old to safely have children so she made his adult kids her own; and the subsequent grandchildren love her to the present day.

The marriage was so blissful, they were clearly soul mates, but the union barely lasted 10 years, when Ernie dropped dead unloading produce from a Cohodas Brothers truck. She was devastated, but his family carried her soul till the healing ensued... She never re-married, and up till recent illness caught up to her, visited his grave daily... he daily walks with her in memory...

The other three listened attentively... This is your Erich Segal's "Love Story" (1972) 'cept the soulmate didn't die of cancer barely one year into the union. My own uncle Orville Haszel, first Marine division, Guadacanal, Marshall Islands, Truk, Leyte Gulf [WWII], had a similar situation meeting Elsie (Howard?) after age 60 and he and the widow lived happily for a scant 10 years. Till one night her heart gave out or was it due to the Superior belt line? Her sons love Orville to this day and moved him closer to them on Highway C Waupaca.

So, she fell in love with him, wanted to be near him, waited with what seemed to be forever to marry him, and daily sees him in her dreams which no other man will ever fulfill in her lifetime... A love story for the ages...

I often wonder in my long daily walks if *She* really understands just how very much I love her beyond the sexual attraction, How devoted I'll be in waiting for her, how terrified I am that she'll send me away and how right up to the last breath I take, she'll be the last thing on my mind...

Chapter 6

Ghosts of Christmases Past and other enduring memories

Last Christmas night I stood at my Mother's grave in the gathering darkness. I looked at the Sinkula's century old farmstead and the other ones that surrounded it. 2007 was a terrible year: the loss of my Mother, the loss of a lady who I was so sure was to have been my soul mate, life threatening illness with my brother and sister in law... serious illness with myself... the realization that while I'd cheated death at least 19 times, I now can't determine if I have the strength or even the desire to make it an even 20.

A terrible recollection from 1970 overtook me when our Green Beret and Vietnamese Special Forces patrol nearly blundered into a fatal ambush and while laying down covering fire for my retreating unit, I discovered I was now cut off and being pursued by North Vietnamese. As I fled, I silently called out for my Mother's help way back then, just as I found myself doing out of loneliness at her grave this Christmas last. For I'm only human, and loneliness in the end turns out to be the worst enemy of each of us as we confront our own mortality and face an uncertain future.

The agility of the human mind to move from image to another is truly astounding. My memory of fear changed to one of sadness. I recalled what had happened in June 2002 with my brother Robert. It was a hot summer's day around ninety degrees. I suddenly felt the need to see him and cheer him up, if only for an hour. There was no time now to mow the lawn, it would have to wait. Robert's chemo-therapy had begun earlier in the week. He had chemo-therapy before. Two years ago in 2000 and almost died from it.

Robert has never shown many feelings for me, even when I almost died in Vietnam, and neither have his two wives. They have all been so thoroughly wrapped up in themselves and when any attention has been paid to me, it has been to berate me. If the situation were reversed and I was the one receiving chemotherapy, he'd stay and cut the lawn instead. I know him that well; he is my one surviving brother.

I remembered my journey that day to see Robert. Driving into the sun, I passed the Smidel old farm where a 40 pounds turkey bird wrecked my first Ford Ranger and nearly me. The road was narrow with barely enough room for two vehicles to pass one another. Suddenly, approaching a junction at 42 South and BB, I saw a brown Montana van. Was it going to stop and yield or hadn't they seen me? Should I go left of center and provide an extra margin of avoidance for both of us? I braked and instinctively I looked to read its license plate. I remember it was 625-AGK. That came from my training as a Sheriff. My heart was sinking, but the van did make an emergency full stop.

Brother Bob told me to leave Kewaunee behind. Don't stay for those who can't or want love you but yet be willing to call you with you for their own self-esteem or just take financial advantage of you. How right you are big brother... God love and keep you... But how do you convince my aching heart? Suppose I'll lose him too... Now we were bonding as maybe both lives are winding down... Why did we wait so long anyway? Life is way too short...

And hours later I drove by her... Running on the shoulder... And two babes with the blown kiss. And a return look that told me you will never be... that I must move away... If I want any happiness or peace...

The Girl of My Dreams

Who says you cannot experience your dreams in real life? After all, have I not dreamed of someone for over five decades, "for someone to watch over me". The song of the 1960s went:

"The girl of my dreams is the sweetest girl. Of all the girls I've known ... each sweet co-ed like a vapor trail.. fades in the after-glow. The brown of her eyes, the black jet of her hair, are a blend of the night-time sky and the moonlight beams on the girl of my dreams. She's the sweetheart of of Sigma Chi."

Didn't I perform that song beautifully at the KHS spring concert. I lost my fear of performing in public that night. The applause went on for a long time. Yea, I nailed it. I lost my fear of performing before an audience that night.

Good Ghosts of Christmases past

Why, Dear God, do things sometimes go to a worst state of Hell on Earth? Pulling myself together and away from this thought, I fought to focus elsewhere and thought of happy family times of my childhood. I remembered "Billy the Brownie". I remember it being broadcast on the radio (WTMJ - AM 560) 5 to 5.15 pm from 1950-1954 and it came from Schuster's Department Store in downtown Milwaukee. My childhood innocence believed it all for about three years and then after the shock of realizing it was not credible, I simply enjoyed it. In those happy days life was sweet, what was there not to love about the world?

Schuster's sponsored "Billy the Brownie" radio show was an excellent marketing strategy to get families to come to their store to "see Santa" and shop while they were there. Every year from Thanksgiving Night to Christmas Day, the fifteen minute radio program was broadcast each weekday at 5:00 pm. The first "Billie the Brownie" radio show was broadcast in 1931 and it ran every year until 1955. The programs contained a mixture of adventure and mystery stories, puzzles, and what was "on special" at Schuster's.

The cast was Santa Claus, his elf Billie the Brownie, Me-tik the Eskimo, Willie Wagtail (Billie's Dog), Fairy Queen, Bongo (Santa's Dog) and sometimes Mrs. Clause via telephone from the North Pole where she would give a full report about how the elves were doing making toys.

The cast played there parts well. Billie the Brownie had a perfect "elf" voice. Mi-Tek, the Eskimo in charge of the reindeer spoke in broken English with grunts. Santa appeared at the end of the show reading letters from children.

The Fox

Mama wore "the Fox" for years at Christmas. Her siblings made it a joint wedding gift on Armistice Day in 1931. A full length adult vixen, complete with eyes, opening mouth and claws, and with the world's most beautiful tail. I'd snuggle into it as she wore it atop her wine colored coat and I'd look out at the crèche of the Christ Child amidst the natural balsams. Life was oh so sweet.

[Regarding the fox stole, from 1930s to the 1950s when fox fur coats and fox stoles were popular and politically correct, Wisconsin had Fromm Brothers raising caged foxes. They were a large operation near the small town Thiensville, Wisconsin. Fromm Brothers operated a silver fox ranch with outdoor pens covering several hundred acres. The horse meat used to feed the foxes came from a nearby horse slaughtering plant. There was no shortage of horses as farms in Wisconsin were switching to tractors and, also, there were thousands of mustangs roaming in various places in the United States. Nowadays, the most frequently farmed animal for its fur is the mink. It's fur is softer than that of the fox. The mink is fashionable and exceeds in economic importance the silver fox, sable, marten, and skunk.]

In the late 1950s even after the fox business had declined, Fromm Brother sponsored a Christmas movie on the local TV station. I do not know if Fromm Brothers were still in the fox rearing business. The site of their fox rearing operation had a number of large, expensive houses and other buildings built on it.

My sister Marie and Mum had two hours to set and trim the tree while I was at Grandpa's on Christmas Eve listening to the last episode of "Billy the Brownie" for that Season.

The remaining hour the flock of cats occupied me. Coming into the house, I saw the living room door was closed with the window wreath glowing through the opaque door glass. Supper always lasted way too long and I was lucky the dishes didn't get done first.

So the door would open and I two-hopped to the tree. What pure magic...

Since they knew how much I loved construction machinery (a trip to the Footbridge County Dept. Shop was a real treat!). I would always find a large metal Tonka or Nylint or La France grader, scraper, pay loader or fire truck. And yes the tires weren't today's cheap plastic but rather real rubber with their special aroma. With a shirt and a small toy, my Christmas would be complete, almost...

Age 8 -- 1953 "The hero who was not"

The Braves moved from Boston to Milwaukee in 1953. It was love at first sight and I'd listen to WTMJ Milwaukee radio. Number 41, Eddie Mathews, third base, was an idol only to be exceeded by number 15 Bart Starr, and number five Paul Horning.

During the two-week Summer Catechism, by the Sisters of the Holy Cross, Mishicot, my Aunt Mame and Uncle Frank offered to take me and Joanne, their daughter, to County Stadium for a Wednesday game with the Cubs. I had never been to Milwaukee and never off the farm... What a dream come true. "Can I go?"

"No." It meant losing a day of catechism. "No!" I spunked... begged... pleaded... shouted... skulked (see any of that since knowing me?) And cried. "Heck, no you want go!!"

They went without me. Three days later, the Nuns Sister Mark and Sister Thomas Moore told the account of how I declined a dream come true because of my religion and faith and refusal to miss even one day of instruction. Frank and Mame lived next door to the Holy Cross Convent. The entire class was told what a wonderful caring person I was to have made such a sacrifice and how God will surely reward me.

Well God did something... He made me feel very small and ashamed... cause none of what the nuns said was true... I cried... I was no hero... I felt small.

Worse I sat there and took the praise and didn't tell the truth about my spunkyiness. I didn't decline the accolades. They accepted heroism under false pretenses. I failed. Years later when "Be Right, Be Brave Have Faith" became my watchwords, I remembered back to that awful day when I didn't tell the truth.

1957

1957 was a good year because the Milwaukee Braves beat the New York Yankees in seven for the World Series. "Beer Town" went bananas. At

61

Wayside Elementary, across from our farm, 1957 saw Milwaukee beat the Yankees in game seven of the World Series and we had listened to every game on the school radio! What a glorious time!

I won the Wayside spelling bee...and lost at KHS with capacity (should be "c" and not "s" for the second c). My savings bank passed $35 and that meant I'd soon have enough to buy a red '57 Chevrolet. I was still dreaming about Betty Sinkula. I was still afraid of Grandpa and "Bozo". Dad wouldn't take me fishing or play ball with me.

I remember I fell on wet linoleum and spilled the lettuce dish – and its watery contents... Mama ran out of the pantry to see what the commotion was, slipped in the mess, fell, and broke her arm.

Cousin Mary and I threw tit cups (milking machine insulators) at the pigs and jumped up and down on the board pile laughing while the hogs went nuts thinking they had been given food.

Christmas Day at Grandma Haszel's.

Eight aunts or uncles with their families (well not Ethel Mae – they were in Virginia and came out only in summer and Ellen Jean being a kind of "Black Sheep" rarely showed). Still, we had a house full and Grandma fried White Rock or Leghorn Roasters. The siblings gathered round the old pump organ and sang. The grandkids then joined in, I didn't realize the terribly sad life that lay ahead, but I knew early on that God gave me the best voice of the next generation Haszel clan and I'd always put it to a good use.

We'd stop off at Uncle Delvin Hershfield's and take him some food. He was my godfather and I'd always get a neat model boat or airplane kit set to assemble.

Christmas night wound down and we would wait to see if Daddy's sister Frances would show. They came from Kewaunee only at Christmas Day and Father's Day. Frances disliked Mama, and turned away from her on her deathbed, for no reason. How can some people hate the very ones they were meant to love?

One Christmas, Daddy was in tears, how rare, "You crazy kids you". My brother Bob and my sister Marie (both working now) had given him a Bulova watch that they had saved for. I felt so hollow that I was a 13 year old and had no money with which to contribute to Daddy's present.

I remember my childhood Christmases well and also ones from years later, two Christmases in Vietnam. French Mass at the Saigon Catholic Cathedral, then the Christmas Eve re-supply of the nuns' schools and orphanages at Ban Me Thuot. Would the Vietcong honor the Cease Fire? If they hadn't, I'd never be here writing these accounts. We were so out-gunned and seriously in harm's way.

Years later, in the 1980s, for some reason I always remember Bob Pietroski (car dealership owner) playing Santa. I remember going with my mother to Washington Park. It was lit only with Christmas lights. Santa's deer sleigh was "in flight" at Washington Park; and magically, as if on cue, the snow would begin to fall. And at the north terminus stood the Parish of Sacred Heart, the steeple bathed in lustrous white light. "God's in His Heaven. All's Right with the world." But that was then, and now a Walgreen's has replaced the long demolished church.

"Hans" Schmidt can't shoot...

Wayne Schmidt was named "Hans" by me. His folks, Duane and Lorraine, had cows, acreage and machinery threefold over the Hineshes.

63

But we had three strong backs: Arthur, Robert, and me. And they needed manpower... so it seems like I spend 75% of the Summer harvesting crops there and 25% at home. Very little recreation: no 4 H, Stars of Carlton, Little League, Braves games in Milwaukee (there's a separate story about that). Just work all summer.

Grandpa ("The Kaiser"), said hard work gave you a much better Heavenly reward. Funny thing though... He only wanted to drive a tractor, never pulling a hay fork rope, nor working in the mows, nor milking cows, nor shocking corn or grain...

Hans (Wayne) was four years younger with a penchant for gravy bread (he'd literally shout for it at the kitchen table till he got it. Goes without saying he was a little Fatty Arbuckle"). But I put up with his "spoiled rabbit" antics. Cause he was the only close neighbor kid. Come summer, the apple trees bore small fruit... then larger fruit. As the rack ones fell (sometimes we helped the harvest by shaking the tree – boy did I catch holy hell for that... for there went the apple butter!)

So anything on the ground (regardless of how it got there) was fair game. We'd bat them with sticks into the hog yard and made the pigs happy while we were Eddie Mathews and Henry Aaron hitting homers. Then we played war soldiers and pretended rotten apples were hand grenades. Splat, splat, splat! How many shirts were ruined after a couple days of hiding them from Mama. How many bruise marks on our faces from direct hits. How many tears from Wayne when my aim was right and a rotten piece of fruit adorned his mug. And, yes, Hans Schmidt couldn't shoot. I could !

Will she and I have our own memories someday?

Christmas Eve, barefooted, she ran through the snow into my arms. I told her quietly what I had felt for the past twenty-five years, and she said she loved me too. Her brothers and her Dad offered so much hope. I did everything with my vows and seven beautiful words. But others in her family have taken away her right to choose and now she is destined to remain just a bittersweet memory from somewhere along my way.

Chapter 7

Requiem and Reminiscences:
St Joseph's of Norman, Wisconsin

Everything earthly has a time line: beginning, middle and end. For our dear, primarily Bohemian, farming parish this time-line had its inception in roughly 1864 and its official end on Saturday, June 20, 2010. St. Joseph's church was an integral part of me. Sadly it is no longer there. The building will remain but it has been decommissioned as a church.

This church building was literally the bedrock of my faith. Memories of it were with me in Vietnam on that wonderful Christmas Eve with the Nuns in 1969... and to that horrible Halloween eve in 1970 when our patrol of 64 was in danger of ambush on the Ho Chi Minh Trail while looking for enemy supplies and transit routes. But God was there.

I lament the fact that after four generations of my Hinesh family being buried in Norman Cemetery with ceremony from St. Joseph's Church, this will not happen for me, a fifth generation Hinesh.

As part of the USgenweb project to provide free genealogy and family history online, volunteers Bev. Diefenbach, Eileen Slaby, and Judy Srnka, on Sept. 11, 1976 transcribed records from headstones in St. Joseph's Catholic Church Cemetery. I have reproduced the Hinesh family entries:

St. Joseph's Catholic Church Cemetery, Kewaunee County, WI

Location: In the village of Norman, 1/4 mile from the corner of Highway G and Norman Road. In the SW 1/4, SW 1/4 Section 16, on Norman Road.

> HINESH:
> Mother/Anna/1854?1937/On the Same Stone With (ossw).
> Father/Frank/1848?1924
> Anton/Jan. 17, 1842/Aug. 7, 1922/ossw;
> Mary/his wife/Sept. 28, 183?/Apr. 7, 1919
> Mayme M./1910?/ossw;
> Frank G./1901?1971
> Donald/1934-/ossw;
> Frances/Mother/1880?1930/ossw;
> Frank/1878-1971/next to;
> Donald Arthur/Apr. 20, 1934/June 6, 1934

I snuggled up in Mother's fox

Midnight Mass: 1948. I am 3 years 9 months. It's cold in the church but beautiful. All the green trees with fragrances and lights. I snuggled up tightly against Mama...she's wearing "THE FOX" (a full adult vixen with its paws, eyes, tail, teeth, and nails). In 1931 at her November wedding in St. John's of Krok, her Haszel siblings presented her with this beautiful fur along with the Lane Cedar Chest. Over the nearly thirty years she lived with me I often brought it downstairs to her... also to the nursing home during the last four years of her life... and one final time to the cherished memories at her wake in 2007.

And I always found mother fox - my vixen. And I danced around the upstairs room with her and regretfully had to put her back till next time – or when Momma wore her again. This August last month I brought her to Mama's new home. Mama remembered and cried. And then the only woman I've loved more than Mama wrapped Mother Fox round her beautiful neck and gorgeous black tresses. And inside I shed tears of pure joy.

Age 4: 1949 Mother in Church With the Fox

Midnight mass 1949, clear and cold. Orion, the mighty Hunter (star constellation), shines with all the brilliance in his beacons Riegel and Betelgeuse. I've just gotten a Ny-Lint orange road grader.

It's after midnight. Mass will go to 1:15 am... I'm getting sleepy, Dad is on the end, Mom, me, Bob (can't sing a lick... that Bozo). Marie is up in the choir singing Silent Night as a solo she had a good voice, but I have better, as good as Mom. But I have a stronger one.

In the small St. Joseph's Church in Norman, a tired little boy nestles up to his mother's breast in her dated wine colored coat with flannel collar. But here's the treat: midnight masses are of the rare treats and times when mom brings the Fox to Church. The full mother Fox (vixen) I have lovingly kept stored in the cedar chest. It's been there since 1931 when her eight brothers and sisters gave it to her for her wedding.

With no fur collar, mom wraps the mothers fox around her neck and breasts. It hooks tip of nose to rear paws. The long tail hangs magnificently. I snuggle into it and peer out at the lighted Xmas trees and beautiful Nativity scenes. I have never been more at peace in this ripe age of four. Life is good, so is God. I pray.

Mama is so Nasty

Daddy was never healthy. This sad and painful memory is from Summer 1949. Daddy fell asleep a lot. He was always tired and had trouble with his feet.

On a hot summer High Mass Day, he fell asleep during the sermon (something he had done on other occasions) and started to snore. Mama gave him a good poke in the ribs, waking him. Sympathizing with my father, I uttered "Mama is so nasty". The whole church heard it. Everyone laughed but not Mama.

People Look East

Remember that old and not often sung Christmas carol? Leaving midnight mass in 1950, there were three hills to climb to reach our 80 acre

70

dairy beyond the Carlton Town Hall. Marie (my sister) was in the choir and Bob (my brother) served at Mass, so we were amongst the last to leave.

Perhaps "The Rosary" is the main reason I'll die Catholic tho' so many of my contemporaries have left the Faith. Looking and driving east that clear and cold (now December 25th) night, I looked upon a living moving Rosary of scarlet red tail lights that is, of a mile of vehicles that preceded that preceded us Eastward... and homeward. And I enjoyed that blessed scene over and over for many Midnight Masses thereafter.

Did Jesus wreck our Chevy?

When Anton Zeise towed our '26 Buick home (7 miles) with his team of horses in 1948, we got our first new car: a '48 Chevy Sedan with a whistling handbrake. How I loved that car tho' I was never to drive it. One cold and icy January Sunday of 1951, I was kept home from Mass with a sore throat and earache. My family returned shaken and in deep anguish. The highway had not been sanded. Several cars lost control down Walechka's Hill, going eastward home. The '48 Chevy was last in line but still had serious front end damage. Heartbroken, I wailed "you went to worship Jesus! Did He cause this?" This was the first painful memory I was to have as to how many bad things happen to very good people who have the best of intentions...throughout my life I've seen that sad and painful scenario played out time and time again... for reasons known but to God.

71

A Good Catholic Boy I Was Not

The Nuns from Holy Cross in Mishicot visited our parish each summer to school us in Catholicism for two solid weeks. Sister Mathew and Sister Mark were our teachers in 1953. Uncle Frank and Auntie Mame wanted to take me and Cousin Joanie to a Saturday Milwaukee Braves game...to see the likes of Danny O'Connel, Johnny Logan, Billy Bridon, Eddie Matthews, Hank Aaron, Joe Adcock, Wes Covington, Del Crandal, Warren Spahn, Lew Burdett and Bob Buehl. (It goes without saying what a fan I was, being able to recite the starting line-up and three pitching aces from memory fifty-seven years later!)

One problem: going to the game meant skipping a training day with the Sisters. I wanted to make that choice and go to the game but Mom and Dad said "NO". I protested and shed a few tears, but it remained "NO GO". So, I did not get my way and go to the game.

Uncle Frank and Auntie Mame lived by the convent. They told the Nuns I gave up the BIG GAME for their instructions. Next Monday, Sister Mark proclaimed my "decision" saying I was "a Saint in the making". I sat mute, speechless in the classroom and feeling like a rat, knowing that the praise was undeserved. It was an experience that taught me how a hypocrite can be made from unworthy praise.

First Communion: June 1954

I still have the pictures of my First Communion when I was eight years old. The boys wore long sleeves with bow ties. The girls had white dresses and veils. We walked down the aisle with our parents, one boy/one girl side by side. My partner was my third cousin Gloria Thor who I had fallen in love

72

with. I wondered as we marched out together if maybe someday we'd do it again: as husband and wife. And the conflict in my life of celibate priesthood versus having a soul mate wife manifested itself and does to the present day, making me realize the issue will out live my relatively short span of life.

Sound of the Guns

I hated Memorial Day solely because we had to carry small flags and march with them to the cemetery. Three volleys of gunfire from the Carlton American Legion terrified me for years. Little did I realize that one day I'd become a hunter and more importantly in the not to distant future I'd leave Kewaunee and go to a far and distant land and serve my country for almost three years. The innocence of childhood and my youth would be forever left behind. General Douglas MacArthur once said that "Old Soldiers Never Die, they just Fade Away." I say "Memories of St. Joseph will never die... they'll see the light of Eternity. May God Bless".

Midnight Mass

There are so many happy memories of my family's parish church, St. Joseph's of Norman. First, I was an altar boy, later a Choir singer, *Silent Night* was my solo. I'd always do a 5th verse in near perfect German. God rest dear Franz Gruber, author. Years later in college I'd duo "Sleep Holy Babe" with Sally Ann Mary Kenney. Many thought we would become a couple, but Sally did not.

We would be about the last to leave the church. We headed East homeward in the black 1948 Chevy. The trips home after Mass meant climbing three hills ahead, Walecka, Blohowiaks and Skarvans, hills ahead. The road east was lined with cars with red taillights like beatitudes of Rosary beads.

Ad sponsored by Debeers Diamond Trading Council: There are two things in life that last forever . .

There are two things in life that last forever. Once again the most beautiful TV ad played itself out for me as I fed mama yogurt last night:

A young, very attractive, Jewish couple fresh from a hissy-fit walked down a sunny Lane. Arms crossed, slightly fuming. She stealing agitated glances at him. Both keeping their lateral distance apart from one another.

With a beautiful violin melody playing, they simultaneously looked up and find they are overtaking a tottering elderly Jewish couple. He moving slowly with a cane, she hanging onto him as her most precious possession next to the Torah, so very much in love for so long.

The young couple splits to walk around the elders. They both glance back at the loving pair and see themselves 50, 60 years hence. There lateral distance eases. They clasp hands and exchange their mutual smile which stays, 'forever'. The ad fades to black with two white sentences, the first is this chapter's title, the second is "love is one of them".

Don't know if "She" recollects seeing it but I pray that ad becomes "us" in mid age now and many years down the road as we advance our journey towards forever. You and me were against the world.

74

Musings on the Fox and the magical cedar chest

Today the magical cedar chest standing in my North upstairs bedroom, covered with dozens of Scale Model farm tractors. There are one hundred in my collection and NASCAR racing cars and trucks (three dozen plus).

Yet on those nights of peaceful dreams, I am back in the South upstairs bedroom of the old log farmhouse, torn down in 1988 after standing 125 to 150 years, and I take out the treasures: old sweaters, mitty's, earmuffs, scarves, an old hot water bottle with tubes what's that doing in here? I savor the rich cedar smell in my dreams and it's much the same when I open it today.

Who says you can't experience her dreams in real life? After all haven't I dreamed of someone for five decades, plus?... for someone to watch over me... for as the song of the 60s went: the girl of my dreams is the sweetest girl... Of all the girls I've known... Each sweet co-ed like a vapor trail... Fades in the afterglow. The Brown of her eyes, the jet black of her hair area, a blend of the nighttime sky... And the moonlight beams on the girl of my dreams. She's a sweetheart of Sigma Chai... Didn't I perform that song wonderfully and KHS Spring concert 1963... How long the applause lasted. Yea I nailed it (to use a gymnastic term) I also stuck it.

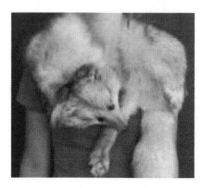

75

I lost my fear of performing that night and I always found Mother Fox, my Vixen. And I danced around the upstairs room with her and regretfully put her back till next time or until Mama wore her once again. This August last I bought her to Mama's new-home. Mama remembered and cried and then the only woman I've truly loved more than Mama wrapped Mother Fox around her beautiful neck and gorgeous black tresses. And inside I shed tears of pure joy.

Chapter 8

_____

People and Politics

I fought for democracy and freedom. I have peace of mind knowing that I did nothing wrong in the Vietnam war. I was a soldier acting under orders. It does not prevent me though, from sometimes being haunted by the horrors of war that I experienced.

It took a while to adjust coming back from Vietnam and to begin my career in the civilian world. Thoughts of having a professional career in the military were there but I had been medevaced out of Vietnam and with disabilities from Agent Orange that weighed against it. It is fortunate I have been able to build on the strengths of my military training and experience. Undoubted it served me well in my work for the Kewaunee Sheriff's Department. Nowadays I am a retiree and I see myself as a volunteer "civil affairs officer" involved in caring for my Kewaunee community.

The Oneida Nation

A call for political action came in 2009. Proposed changes in legislation at the state level would have an adverse effect in my community. No longer would my high school be allowed to use the name "Indians" for its sports teams. In particular, the Wisconsin State Senate's proposed Bill 25 was a direct attack on the 5,000 years of Oneida cultural heritage which was celebrated in Kewaunee. Papers that I prepared arguing against the passing of this bill can be found in Appendices 8.1 and 8.2. My personal communications to a state senator can be found in Appendices 8.3 and 8.4.

Sadly, my efforts and representations for my community and especially friends in the Class of 1963 Kewaunee High School alumni were unsuccessful. I knew at the outset that I had a very slim chance of succeeding with my campaign but I believed, and still do, that it was worthwhile to express my views and those of many others in my community.

The new Wisconsin law establishing a procedure for challenging a school board's use of a race-based nickname, logo, mascot, or team name went into effect May 20, 2010. It did allow the continued use of "Indians" as a mascot and team name by Kewaunee High School, but if there was a complaint filed and it was ratified by the State Department of Public Instruction that a new name would need to be found.

It was a fight worth fighting and one we might have won because many Senators in Wisconsin were opposed to the new law and others might have been swayed giving our side the majority vote. There were additional arguments that we had more than enough laws and did not need another, and that local communities could responsibly decide for themselves about their mascot and team nicknames.

A complaint was made by a school district resident under Act 250 (as it was known then). In November 2010 the name "Indians" was dropped and replaced by "Storm". I do say that I am happy that the new name was democratically selected by the current students of Kewaunee High School, young people who shall lead us into the future. Additionally, the name

"Storm" is a part of nature and one which is as relevant to Native Americans and the Oneida Nation as it is to anyone else in our farming community. We'll all get used to it after a while. My argument still remains that there was no need to change the name from "Indians" to "Storm". I have provided reflections about Wisconsin banning Native American symbolism in Appendix 8.6.

My interest in politics is not restricted to local issues. I follow the news about national and international issues.

War, People and Politics

The best reason I can give against war is the death and destruction it brings means that the souls of innocent children, grandchildren, great and great-great grandchildren will never walk on Earth. It destroys the "family" aspect of family values. The Old Testament it is describes Cain killing his brother Abel. Cain's legacy today is "war", striking down others on the field of battle and causing their death, taking them away from their family and those who love them.

I went to Vietnam because my high school classmate Terry Neumeier and eleven other Kewaunee County combatants did not return alive. I wanted their sacrifices to have served a purpose and in the end not to have been in vain. I believed in McNamara's theory that if Vietnam fell, then Cambodia, Laos, Thailand, Burma, Malaysia, the Philippines, and Indonesia would follow like so many falling dominoes. The line was drawn in Vietnam to stem the Communist tide for once and for all.

There was a precedent for this, as we had maintained South Korea at the 38th parallel and Communism went no further. Of course we kept the

U.S. 8th Army there, without which I think the North Koreans (the Commies) would have taken the whole of Korea within weeks of our departure. A similar precedent was in Europe when N.A.T.O. (North Atlantic Treaty Organization) prevented the Russians from expanding their communist empire. With its military power, Russia could easily have extended all the way west in Europe to the Rock of Gibraltar and the Atlantic Ocean. It is thanks to the U.S. 7th Army and the U.S. Air Force and Navy this did not happen. Communists respect only one thing: counter-military force, they make their promises and then break them.

A major case in point is the Paris Peace Accords of 1972. Suan Tuy and Le Duc Tho assured us in writing that the DMZ (De-militarized Zone) would be maintained in the new Vietnam and we'd get all our Prisoners of War (P.O.W.S.) back. We'd have full diplomatic relations and the United States would not be obligated to pay war reparations, but "all our troops must be gone". That's when the war turned. Henry Kissinger and President Nixon had taken command and we left. We left "lock, stock and barrel."

What did the Vietnamese Commies do? They bided their time, did not re-invade next week, month or even year; but on April 30th, 1975 the Gold Star on Red flag flew over **Saigon** (it was promptly renamed **Ho Chi Minh City**). The simple lesson was: take out the U.S. covering forces and in came the Commies like an invasion of wharf rats.

What does this lesson teach us for Iraq and for United States policy in the Middle-East? I do not know, other than to say, if we leave now the whole Middle-East loses along with us. I believe that invading Afghanistan and fighting the al-Qaeda and the Taliban was a justifiable war against terrorism after 9/11.

Iraq seemed to be a revenge war against Saddam who tried to have President George Bush the first killed. There were other reasons too. There's the part British Intelligence played, initiating fears about a drainage pipe bomb rocket launcher and chemical warfare. There have been claims that British Intelligence misled United States intelligence. No "weapons of mass destruction" were found in Iraq. But there was justification for invading Iraq and it has become clearer as more information is discovered about the atrocities and oppression Saddam Hussein's regime inflicted on Iraq's citizens.

Have my political views changed since I volunteered for Vietnam? Would I serve in Iraq if called? I'd leave tonight. I am much older and do not have the same mental alertness and physical fitness that I had when I served in Vietnam. But, I have experience, maturity, and combat smartness. I would serve my Country well to the best of my abilities, the same as I did in Indo-China. If I was needed for a particular role I would have no hesitation in taking it.

Peace, People and Politics

Is it possible to establish a long lasting and international peace? The road to that can come from ending tribalism and improving the economies and quality of life for all. I have heard it said that history is not established truth and that every few decades it is re-examined, re-evaluated and re-written. By invading Iraq, President George Bush the Second has helped change the Middle East forever. It is difficult, but Iraq has been set on a path towards democracy, freedom and human rights. I do not believe that history will see the invasion of Iraq as a mistake.

There are many Americans, some of them Vietnam veterans, working as contractors in Afghanistan and Iraq. Many are businessmen with a track record of success and are using their skills to create a business infrastructure that can successfully participate in the modern day world economy. It is a formidable task. Vietnam was different. They had been colonized by the French and had integrated positive parts of French culture.

There were more than 70,000 foreign workers in U.S bases in Iraq and Afghanistan. Some services that formerly were provided by American military personnel are now done by nationals of other countries. General McChrystal in Summer 2010 drew attention to the plight and problems created by outsourcing services and using foreign workers. American freedom of speech enables this information to be broadcast. It can bring about change to right things that are wrong.

Thanking is Good but Understanding is Better

Saying "Thanks" compares to saying "I love you" in that it's better late than not at all. Hopefully the future will bring final healing that has eluded so many of us Vietnam Veterans for over forty years now. For many veterans the scars of Vietnam have lay primarily in that some of our fellow countrymen have not accepted us, shunned us and even vilified us as war criminals in some instances. With very rare exceptions, I do not believe any war crimes were committed. When I left in my 3rd year of volunteer service in Vietnam, I had witnessed no war crimes committed by Americans, nor was I aware of any. I believe that as in all past wars, some did happen, but in no greater proportion and more likely much less than in wars past.

Many fellow Vietnam Veterans have been much worse off than I, many turning to illegal controlled substances and alcohol. Many, like I, have "survivors guilt" to the present day, tormented by the loss of so many buddies and wondering over and over again why we cheated death but they made the ultimate sacrifice, and what right we have to live while they had to die. We have so many restless nights, without peace. Dreams of lost comrades and combat torment us and perhaps always will. This is what needs to be understood about us. We had to reinvent our lives upon our return home and some of us are still trying.

Militarily, we could have had the success in Vietnam, that we ultimately enjoyed in South Korea. But politically we were doomed and had no choice but to leave lest our homeland descend into anarchy and civil war as in centuries past. At least that did not happen and to some degree America has healed from the scars of the Vietnam War.

Please remember that we didn't have an all volunteer force like we have now. We had the draft. Most Vietnam Veterans, unlike myself, didn't volunteer... they were inducted via conscription and the draft. Some evaded but the vast majority served their time and did their best under difficult military circumstances with sections of the public back home not understanding or appreciating them.

Vietnam was the worst of times since the American Civil War in that this country was nearly again torn asunder. Caught in the throes of the Cold War, many like myself believed that we were protecting America from international Communism and that the fall of South Vietnam meant the fall of all Indo-China, Southeast Asia, Indonesia and the Philippines. And so we did our very best to defend the U.S.A and freedom in the world.

As in Bible Scripture (and in the Byrd's rock hit... "Turn, Turn, Turn") it was "A Time To Heal", regardless of our feelings for Vietnam. The same applies to Afghanistan and Iraq. We need to give 100% acknowledgment and support to our fine women and men in the military who have served to protect us, who have put themselves "In Harm's way". They should be treated with dignity and helped to find jobs after they leave military service.

Number plates

The plate jumped out from the "dirty Ford freestyle" **64 WIS** ... I all but saluted it. One of the top five I've ever seen along with wings. Battleship Wisconsin. USS Wisconsin (BB64) was launched in 1943 at Philadelphia, PA: five battle stars in the Pacific, dozens of Kamakazee kills providing anti-air cover for carriers. Recalled in 1954 for Korea. It was hit by a Korean shell while firing off Pyongyang... no one was killed... Thank God.

USS Wisconsin (BB-64)

I had to know! Did he serve on the ship that day? I waited by the Leicester library. I knew it was him, the second he came out the door. An older version of me. Fifteen or twenty years older. Pushing 80... proud and grateful to be alive... Like me.

Please tell me, sir. Were you aboard when the north Koreans straddled her? Yes, said he. How far offshore? About 10 miles. Why didn't you folks stand off out of range, sir? Son, we were firing inland targets nearly 10 miles from shoreline. I'm used to telling the details of what happened.........

What a miracle... I replied. The biggest US battle wagon and the only one hit without fatalities.

Yes son, it was a miracle. Now, explain your plate to me?

Five minutes later he was gone. I and my plate had certainly met its match, and the feeling glowed deep and warm... From across the historical wars... Comrades in arms, shared, smiled, exchange history, understood, and parted happier for having met and communicated their times.

Chapter 9

_____

A Clinical Perspective on Post Traumatic Stress Disorder

by Dr. Sonja Raciti, Clinical Psychologist

Throughout Mark's life story you can see the impact that both farming and Vietnam has had on him. Vietnam first became important to him during his days in ROTC when two of his close comrades were killed in action and it has in many ways held him captive for over 40 years following combat. He described their deaths being his turning points. Turning points often occur when tragedy has struck home. We saw this after 9-11-2001 when both men and women who had previously never considered a military career began enlisting and filling the ranks in all branches of our military due to renewed patriotism, anger, or hurt. Many of them had friends or family members who lost their lives to terrorism. Most Americans began feeling an increase in pride in our country which was easily seen by flags being proudly hung outside of homes, media reporting and even changes in our music and TV shows.

War usually makes people feel a loss of control and powerless, especially when the losses are personal such as in Mark's case. Anger, hurt and sadness become enmeshed with the desire to make the other person's sacrifice count. No soldier wants to die for nothing. Standing up and becoming part of the fight enables people to feel useful and it lessens the overwhelming feelings of helplessness. In Mark's case this fueled his desire to excel in ROTC and to join the officer ranks serving in Vietnam and for him to give up his aspirations of continuing the family tradition of farming despite his obvious love for the land.

Posttraumatic Stress Disorder (PTSD) is a serious and debilitating trauma induced disorder. The long-term effects of war trauma has been something we have written about and spoken about for centuries now. It has been called many things depending on the decade and war. After the civil war you can find references for soldier's heart, which then progressed to combat fatigue or shell shock after World War I and to battle fatigue or gross stress reaction after World War II. The American Psychological Association did not formalize a diagnosis until 1980 when they began calling it Posttraumatic Stress Disorder or PTSD. Due to the tardiness in recognizing the potentially short and long-term effects of trauma, often times soldiers prior to 1980 with these symptoms were seen as mentally weak and or as cowardly. Many of these same soldiers did not receive any treatment which resulted in a large percentage of them self-medicating with alcohol and drug use. We continue to see many Vietnam War veterans suffer from both PTSD and addiction in today's society and many of them succumbed to homelessness in part due to the trauma of war impairing their ability to function successfully in a non-combat environment.

Currently in order to meet criteria for PTSD, a person must have been exposed to a catastrophic event involving actual or threatened death or injury to oneself or others around them. The person's response to the event must involve intense fear, helplessness or horror and in children this can be experienced as disorganized or agitated behavior.

PTSD is categorized as a severe anxiety disorder that can develop after exposure to any event that results in psychological trauma. The trauma then overwhelms the individual's ability to cope with life stressors. A clinically significant amount of people react to trauma, however we normally see a decrease in trauma symptoms within the first 3-6 weeks. PTSD is only diagnosed after 30 days have elapsed from the time of the event. In the case of on-going trauma such as the case with war or abuse, PTSD can be diagnosed a month after the first occurrence if diagnostic criteria is met. In some cases symptoms arise months or even years after the initial trauma and it is then diagnosed with delayed-onset.

Symptoms for PTSD include re-experiencing the original traumatic event(s) through recurrent and intrusive recollections of the event, active avoidance of stimuli associated with the trauma and numbing of general responsiveness, and increased arousal symptoms. Re-experiencing of trauma can be through flashbacks and/or nightmares. Intense psychological distress or physiological reactivity can occur when the person is exposed to events which resemble or symbolize the traumatic event for them. Often the triggering events are only meaningful to them and on the surface are mundane things (for example, certain cologne for a woman who was raped, trash lying by the road side by current soldiers who have seen IED's explode in Iraq or Afghanistan). The person often makes a deliberate choice to avoid certain stimuli because they trigger such an intense surge of anxiety symptoms. Many soldiers coming back from combat will avoid crowded areas including places of worship, malls, grocery stores, etc. Loud noises such as fireworks cause severe startle responses. At the same time, diminished responsiveness to the external world is common. The person is no longer interested in doing the same activities as before and they feel emotionally disconnected from others. Some people experience reduced ability to feel emotions, especially related to intimacy, tenderness and

91

sexuality. Some people begin to see themselves as having a foreshortened future. Symptoms of increased arousal may include sleep disturbance, increased startle response, hyper-vigilance and increased irritability and/or outbursts of anger. People frequently have difficulty completing tasks and/or concentrating due to their mind wandering back to the trauma event. Symptoms must be present for more than one month and they must cause clinically significant distress or impairment in social, occupational, or other important areas of functioning.

People with PTSD are at a higher risk to experience further psychological symptoms which can then result in comorbid disorders. They are at increased risk of Panic Disorder, Agoraphobia, Obsessive-Compulsive Disorder, Social Phobia, Specific Phobia, Major Depressive Disorder, Somatization Disorder, Sleep Disorders and Substance-Related Disorders to name a few. PTSD symptoms are very distressing to the person and frequently to people they are in relationships with. Suicidal ideation is frequently reported and the rate for completed suicide is much higher than amongst the normal population.

Survivors guilt is one of the hallmarks of PTSD and soldiers in combat frequently wonder why they were chosen to continue to live and not the other person/people. Religious beliefs and spirituality are called into question, which oftentimes results in loss or change of an individuals core beliefs. Guilt has a way of digging itself deep into the inner workings of yourself and enmeshes with your sense of self and the way you begin to view the world. Many trauma survivors become addicted to alcohol or drugs as a way of quieting that inner voice and the overwhelming feelings which then perpetuates their feelings of guilt and self-blame.

Risk factors for developing PTSD are: increased timeframe of traumatic event(s), number of events, higher severity of trauma experienced, having mood instability prior to traumatic event, abuse history dating back to early childhood, or having poor social support. Mark did experience several traumatic events which were longer in duration; however he did have a good social support system, a strong desire to help others and he was raised in a loving and caring environment. On average, children, adolescents and females seem to be more susceptible to PTSD. Typically children who have PTSD were physically, sexually and/or emotionally abused by caregivers and with adult women, we most frequently see females who were victims of domestic violence and/or sexual assault/rape.

What makes one person experience the debilitating symptoms of PTSD while another person can experience the same trauma and function normally afterwards? Overall this is still a mystery, however we have recently began finding some answers for this question. Fear is triggered by an adrenaline response and in the case of PTSD it is overactive which then creates neurological patterns in the brain which can persist for decades after the actual event. Approximately 70% of people diagnosed with PTSD show a low secretion of cortisol and high secretion of catecholamine in their urine, with a norepinephrine/cortisol ratio consequently higher than comparable non-diagnosed individuals. Normally both the catecholamine and cortisol levels of an individual are elevated after a stressor.

Some researchers have associated the response to stress in PTSD with long-term exposure to high levels of norepinephrine (which is stress hormone) and low levels of cortisol both of which are associated with increased learning ability. What do this actually mean in regards to PTSD? It translates to people with PTSD having a maladaptive learning pathway associated with fear which is hypersensitive, hyper-reactive and hyper-responsive. Low cortisol levels may predisposition individuals to PTSD. Cortisol typically helps restore homeostasis after a stress response which

93

may result in people with low levels experiencing a longer and more distressing response than others.

Vietnam continues to be of significance due to the high amount of war veterans still experiencing PTSD symptoms and this having a huge impact on the rest of their life. In Mark's case Vietnam was a turning point in his life both personally and professionally. He did not experience the full symptoms associated with PTSD, however he did see and experience trauma's which have remained in his psyche and which have continued to shape the person he is today. Mark talked a about still waking up occasionally due to having a nightmare about the tiger which came close to attacking him in the night. He spoke of feelings of both intense fear and feeling responsible for the soldiers who served under him. Serving in the military you are trained to lead soldiers and to make sure all are taken care of under your command. In times of war all of us realize that this is not realistic and that some of the soldiers will not make it home, however that does not make it any easier emotionally to let go. In addition to this, officers often have the responsibility of making sure the mission continues and all soldiers are mentally prepared to continue operations. In the military this means not showing weakness and always remaining a pillar of support for others.

One of the biggest difficulties and some of the greatest losses within combat can occur due to accidents and/or friendly fire. These tragic occurrences can be more difficult for soldiers and family members to cope with due to the unexpected manner of dying and the ramifications that the death was preventable and the person at fault is often a friend. Mark referred to the difficulty of being able to distinguish between enemy and friendly fire and how scary this was for him.

Current treatment for PTSD in the adult population includes Prolonged Exposure Therapy (PE), Eye Movement Desensitization and Reprocessing (EMDR) and Cognitive Processing Therapy (CPT). All three therapy modalities are currently being taught by and used by the United States Department of Defense and the Department of Veterans Affairs and are seen as the gold standard of treatment, meaning that these have been found to have the highest merit based on research findings. All three are weekly treatments which take approximately 12-15 sessions to progress to the point where symptoms are no longer in the clinically significant range. Treatment can be done for newly acquired and or old traumas regardless of how long ago the trauma was. Many war veterans from Vietnam and Korea, Gulf war and the current War on Terror are now seeking treatment and are progressing to having a healthier life.

In Prolonged Exposure therapy, clients are giving the coping skills and the support to verbally and physically relive the traumatic experience within the therapy session repeatedly until their emotional response begins to diminish and normalize. Prolonged Exposure treatment starts with education about treatment, common reactions as well as symptoms you are experiencing. This helps the client understand the goals of the next sessions. Clients are then taught to control their breathing and begin to relax using deep breathing techniques. This helps them remain focused and centered when they begin retelling the trauma that took place. Homework is for the client to listen to the recording of the session and for them to practice going to places or engaging in activities that are safe but they have been avoiding due to these triggering emotional responses. Often times they remind the person of the trauma. The exposure practice allows for clients to feel empowered and in control of their own reactions, while diminishing their feelings of distress.

In Cognitive Processing Therapy clients are asked to rethink the trauma and the way the trauma has influenced their life. Cognitive Processing therapy also begins with an educational component discussing symptoms and treatment. In the next stage, the client is taught how to be more aware of their own thoughts and feelings in regards to the trauma. The therapist helps them to rethink about the trauma in a healthier manner. The client learns strategies to question and/or challenge their thoughts and beliefs, which then helps them to find a better balance between their beliefs prior to the trauma and after the trauma.

EMDR uses bilateral stimulation (right/left eye movement, tactile stimulation, or sound), which repeatedly activates the opposite sides of the brain releasing emotional experiences that are "trapped" in the nervous system. This assists the neuro-physiological system, the basis of the mind/body connection, to free itself of emotional blockages and reconnect itself. In EMDR client and therapist identify different targets for processing. The targets are disturbing past events and/or situations which trigger a negative emotional response. The client then identifies a vivid visual image of the memory, a negative believe about the self which stems from this memory, a preferred positive belief which is ranked according to the clients feeling of valid vs not true, their related emotions which are also rated according to intensity and their body state. Through the use of bilateral stimulation, the client is then able to slowly process the negative emotional states and enhance the positive thoughts. Frequently clients have difficulty putting their thoughts or emotions into words and EMDR allows them to process it through eliminating stored stress responses/feelings in the body.

Mark was fortunate in many ways to have been able to serve his time in Vietnam and return to friends and family back in Wisconsin. However, he did lose many of his comrades and his life changed dramatically from being a farmer to having gone to war and finding a new path for him and his family post war. He successfully moved on to excel as a contributor to his community.

Dr. Sonja Raciti is a Clinical Psychologist in the Child and Adolescence Assistance Center at Schofield Barracks Health Clinic, Honolulu, Hawaii and is Brigade Behavioral Health Officer for 29th BSB Charlie Company Hawaii Army National Guard. She is a faculty member of the graduate program in Clinical Psychology at Argosy University, Honolulu, Hawaii.

Chapter 10

Onward and Upwards

My Final Chapter and My Future

I hope the content of this book has been interesting for my readers and has served different purposes. Educational for my readers as a work that exemplifies the demands of military service and the challenges of returning to my homeland after active duty serving in Vietnam. On another level, it is my analysis of my life and my community. I thank Martin Hackel for writing the Foreword and also for his friendship since my high school days. Also, my thanks to Dr. Raciti for her contributing chapter.

Religious Beliefs

Parts of my book are strongly focussed on how my Catholic faith has guided my actions. Is there advice I would give to others? The essential things are to believe and trust in God. Having a good attitude, being honest and accepting the difficulties and challenges of life are simple rules. I am fortunate and enjoy life. For me, obeying the rules is not difficult. I follow the beliefs of my Catholic faith and teachings of my Church.

What does God do with people who do not obey the rules and destroy the reputation, good name and character, and sometimes even souls, of those they hate? Is salvation and repentance possible for them? What of those harmed so irreparably that they renounce God, go over to the dark side and self-destruct? If a poor soul believes that all the good he has done in his life is for nothing, that his fellow people have renounced all that he did for them and wish him evil, and that God does not love him, then what should he do? What happens if he heeds the words of Job's acquaintance and "curses God and dies"?

The Old Testament teaches us that though he lost his family, friends, career and good name that Job did not "curse God and die" when so advised. Instead he simply said, "Blessed be the name of Yahweh (God)" and by doing this he found both his temporal and eternal life restored". I believe that the mercy of God is infinite.

John Calvin, a protestant preacher in the 1600'ish years believed in "predestination". Does this mean that when we are born God knows whether we will be saved or damned? Does it mean we do not have a free will nor the grace to save ourselves? Does it mean we are powerless to control our own destiny and God does not care? Are we goats, not sheep from the start? Whose example should we follow, Job's or John Calvin's?

The only way I can reconcile Calvin's view of "predestination" is that God has foresight into the passage of time and has knowledge of who by their own free will respond on their own. The election of those who shall believe is not controlled or orchestrated by God; there is power in each individual to choose and follow him.

Undoubtedly, my religious beliefs and values were forged by my parents and the community I lived in. I shall never forget the following story which was told at a 1955 Summer Catechism class by Sisters Matthew and Mark of the Sisters of Holy Cross of Mishicot, Wisconsin (it was the custom of the Sisters to take the names of male Saints). This following story is reproduced as best I can remember it:

Falsehoods and lies are like feathers in the wind.

For years the routine proceeded like clockwork and the changing of seasons and migration of birds: the aging "wag" (gossip) took part in the prescribed routine of monthly private Confession (in past decades it was the routine and not the exception). And she confessed the same sins of calumny, gossip, slander, half-truths, greed, and envy; like a Litany of the Saints, the good Pastor would know what was coming next even before her words were spoken. For years he had heard much the same thing and had dispensed much the same advice before invoking her to recite an act of contrition and "go and sin no more". But Our Father, Hail Mary and Glory Be's weren't "cutting it" for this pitiful woman who in her zeal to promote her importance had irreparably damaged so many innocent souls along the path of life; with, in some cases, their good name was destroyed, and a few were being lost to God and left for Satan in their overwhelming despair. What to do?

From the private confessional, the Priest heard her padding and shuffling her way in with her breathing labored by developing asthma. And then, like dozens of times before, it began once again, the same sins, the same character assassination, the same outpouring of lies and gossip he had heard so many times before.

101

Clearly something had to change. God's will was not being followed and at that point the plans of Satan were being promoted by this pathetic person, but what to do? So the Priest did this: "My child, make if possible a Perfect Act of Contrition (repentance not for fear of Hell, but primarily for having hurt God), go and sin no more, and now for your Penance ...". And then the lightning struck. "Instead of the prayers I have invoked you to say for so many months, I want you to collect a grain basket full of goose feathers from your next pillow tacking and then wait for the day of a westerly wind which whistles in the steeple eaves. You will know when the time is right. Then take your burden of sins which the basket of feathers represents, climb the church stairway to the steeple and through the opening between the bells, discharge your burden to God's four winds by emptying the basket into the breezes. Come back down then and begin your search to retrieve each and every feather. When, and only when, you have located every one, fasten a pillow and bring it to church whereupon offer it as sin reparation to God. Go now in Peace and set forth to your appointed task."

There was total silence, then a few muffled sobs. "But Father, it's impossible to do, one cannot possibly retrieve all the feathers but maybe a few. A west wind will carry many into the lake".

More silence, more sobs, then the Priest spoke, knowing that for the first time in years some contrition was felt: "I know my child that I have given you an impossible task. You see, God knows that, just as you can't locate but a fraction of the feathers, so also you can't restore the good name and character of those many you so grievously harmed with your lies, hurtful gossip, envy and lack of charity. Furthermore people tend to believe the worst and ignore recantations and efforts to restore truth and justice to reputations."

The Sisters didn't tell us if the account had a happy ending or the mean-spirited woman got back on the hard narrow road to salvation. They left us to wonder........

The twice-weekly half-day sessions ended at noon. I biked the mile home and told Mama of that wondrous account that so puzzled me. I asked her what she thought. I remember her words: "Markie, if you really love others and want to help them, you must first promise God never to hurt them by jealous words, angry thoughts or gossip to help yourself but which harms them..."

"FIRST DO NO HARM" was what my mother taught from the time we learned to speak, along with "LOVE ONE ANOTHER" and "MAY GOD BLESS". Three short sentences, ten words in total. The middle sentence, LOVE ONE ANOTHER will be written on my tombstone.

A New Era

Sadly I have no farming legacy to pass on, only a collection of 144 scale model tractors and implements for the Kewaunee County Agricultural Heritage & Resources, Inc. Somehow that seems so inadequate to me, but it's the best I can do (Appendix 10.1 – letter from Jennifer Gozdzialski, Director of Acquisitions).

It's a brief acknowledgement and a cynical one of the potential life as a farmer which was denied to me. One I might have enjoyed.

My Legacy

Every one has "watersheds" and "fork in the road decisions". I described my recollection of very important ones in my first chapter. It is saddens me that I have never found a soul mate, a woman to share life together, and have no children. My experiences in Vietnam, particularly in running a field hospital (a first aid station) had put me in role a similar position to a chaplain consoling injured and dying soldiers. After Vietnam I thought about becoming a priest but I wanted to have a wife and family.

Where have you gone Joe DiMaggio... and all the Sisters too?... More musings...

I saw the two via the Ranger rearview... two elderly Holy Family Convent nuns... by their activity, elderly... one was obese and hobbled. With canes would they see the tiny but foreboding ice patch near Perkins' front door from the overhang drip?

Abruptly stopping and hitting four ways, I run out to alert and assist them in... tipping my cap like all ex-altar boys still do. The warmth of their smiles cheered me into blissful memory that never did I meet a nun I disliked. Perhaps others got 'rulered', or knelt on hard kneelers, in a corner for tomfoolery but never I. All was calm... all is still bright memory wise. To me all nuns were good.

Sometimes in this wasteland of loneliness in which I exist, I muse thusly: Some nuns left their order 'cause they long for men and children. Why didn't destiny allow me to meet one? With both of us being religious, it would have lasted Forever.

Fact remains... Sisters are aging and dying. God love them... why are they not being replaced? Why can't women be priests? Why the damn celibacy? Is Catholicism going the way of the dinosaur?

My Love and Loss

And where is She, My Best friend, and where am I? I say very little to her family... but one day the subject came up with her Dear Dad (who nowadays I probably love more than my late Father... though nonetheless for my own dad I became chief caregiver for and helped have two or more extra years of life) and I simply said, "You realize that I don't want her for sex; I want and need Her Forever... can you believe that?" The one-word reply from this stroke impaired old man said volumes: "Yes"!. Nuff said. Her whole family knows without me telling them. Her vindictive niece is so adept at advertising.

Acknowledgement and Assurance

I like to receive acknowledgment and applause, not in any self-aggrandizing way but as reassurance that others believe I'm doing the right thing and to make life better for my community. It is important that I see I am helping make life better.

To have happiness and a life of fulfilment, faith in an afterlife and being able to sleep soundly knowing I have always tried my best to do the right thing. I am very fortunate.

The Sign Project

The sign project is to recognize and celebrate our young people (with who we all identify and live vicariously, whether we realize it or not). It recognizes the champions, it gives hope to younger siblings and friends who upon seeing this recognition, realize that all things are possible through dedication and hard work and perhaps know that a decade of effort may reap them similar rewards. It certainly makes parents and all relatives proud. It makes opponents pause and reflect as their buses pass these signs and help plant the seeds of doubt that "The Storm" can be weathered. Create doubt in your adversary... it's the beginning of your triumph (old CIA psychology operations principal!)

Glenn Teske, the best of our class of 1963 in my humble opinion, and I each developed this idea, went separately to Kewaunee Mayor John Blaha the same day and then pooled our efforts: development, fundraising, debating and even begging, to "strike while the iron is hot" and *get it done* NOW, not tomorrow, for tomorrow seldom comes on these ideas.

In the 32 years I've lived in Kewaunee I've only seen total unity on two occasions: when Drew Wojtaa and Jamie Bertrand hoisted the Wisconsin D4 foot tall state championship trophy on the gridiron of Camp Randall, Madison on a cold magical November night. And, then during a May-like afternoon when our "Chain of Sisters" all raised that Gold Basketball at the Kohl Center after an unbelievable conquest of Oostburg.

So now Glenn and I wish to capture this "lightning in a bottle" for all time. Perhaps these accomplishments can foster communitywide pride in cooperation on other levels as well. Perhaps it'll prevent cuts in educational budgets and more local aid to our school district should state aids continue to plummet and force us to make really tough choices. For "United we stand... divided we totter".

Somehow this puts the whole debacle of the "Indian Law" and loss of our 1926 – 2010 symbol into a positive perspective. And I'm so glad it started with Glenn and me of the class of 1963. A democracy is only as effective as the lifelong educational process of its people... Especially its schooled students.

Sports Center

My most recent fork in the road decision was prompted by seeing an opportunity where I could do something tangible. And at the same time promote my belief that physical fitness and sports are of great benefit. I decided that I would use the bulk of my savings to implementing the creation of a sports center. I have done this and continue in this mission.

MARK HINESH, center, has named the Build the Future Foundation the beneficiary of his life insurance policy, currently valued at $663,725. He has designated the funds be spent to build a weight room and fitness center at Kewaunee High School. Don Rabas, right, will help in the planning process. Superintendent of Schools Barb Lundgren, left, has met with Hinesh several times to set the parameters of the offer.

A spin-off from the sports center has been to provide facilities to develop soccer as a local sport. Soccer is increasing in popularity and provides an alternative to other sports. I hasten to add that I have not abandoned my Green Bay Packers, a community owned football team with extraordinary success in recent years competing against wealthier NFL teams. I continue to avidly follow their progress.

Pictured above are (Left) George Orr and Mark Hinesh (Right) John Berner and Lou Richards, standing by the new sign that was donated by Mark Hinesh for the Kewaunee Health & Fitness Center

And my local high school team, now the Kewaunee Storm? I am still unhappy about it, but in the space of a few months I got used to this new name and it is now a talking point about the days of my Kewaunee "Indians" and how the name came to be changed.

An Acknowledgement

Heather clapped me on the back and broke into her lovely smile. Mark, I've got the Lincoln girls softball varsity coaching job! Start next week!

I wanted to high-five her but that's pretty hard when she's waitressing carrying hot coffee and eggs over easy. That could get messy. I know how much she's wanted it and I had said a few prayers in hope of her getting this result. Heather is every man's dream, down to earth, very sincere. She's a single mom in her early thirties and I am old enough to be her dad.

Challenges

I am moving into an era of "seniors helping seniors". That's one solution to an increased number of the population requiring elder care due to the baby boomers and people living longer after retirement. A good deal of my time most days is devoted to helping ensure there is sufficient help for seniors in my community.

In this book I have described important aspects of my life. The importance of my childhood experiences, my religious beliefs, my military service, my career, my satisfaction from current achievements, and continuing to meaningfully contribute to my community. I've also raised several controversial and political issues. There's a text-book example of the process of democracy in State and community politics, and not without criticisms of it. It is my believe that a democracy is only as effective as the lifelong educational processes of its people... especially it's school students.

I'd love to hear from former classmates, friends and anyone who would like to comment on my book. What paths have they taken and how are they doing? What are their beliefs and what do they think about how things should be done? I can be contacted by email at:

mark.hinesh@pacificacademic.com

APPENDIX 8.1

Native American Logo Resolution

Native American Logo Resolution. Expressing Kewaunee County's Concern and opposition to State Senate proposed Bill 25 to forbid any and all logos, references, and symbols of Native American culture within Wisconsin State Funded School Districts and the communities wherein they reside.

WHEREAS Senate Bill 25 prescribes compliance failure in any of the twenty-two (22) school districts that currently utilize Native American symbolism to result in financial penalties and State aid forfeitures.

WHEREAS Kewaunee County has been blessed with over 5,000 years of Native American culture, artifacts, and traditions. Concern exists over potential elimination of the ongoing celebration of Native American Culture.

WHEREAS Kewaunee School District is located within sacred burial grounds of the Potawatomi, Oneida, and other tribes.

WHEREAS the Oneida Nation continues to share their rich cultural heritage within Kewaunee School District by conducting Pow-wows and educational lectures.

WHEREAS Kewaunee School District continues to celebrate the rich Native American history by using the symbol of a Shaman Chief as a sign of respect for this ancient and venerable culture.

WHEREAS Kewaunee School District has used a culturally sensitive symbol of a Shaman Chief for nearly a century.

WHEREAS the residents of Kewaunee School District express over 90% opposition to Senate Bill 25. The passage of this bill, as an unfunded political mandate, will promote extreme financial hardship to taxpayers residing within this district.

WHEREAS taxpayers in 22 State School Districts would have to pay for band, sports, and other uniforms, literature and correspondences, signage, and repainting of municipal landmarks which contain Native American symbolism.

NOW THEREFORE, BE IT RESOLVED that residents of Kewaunee School District express overwhelming opposition to Senate Bill 25.

Wisconsin's Fiscal Responsibility if Laws Forbidding Native American Symbols in School Districts are Enacted

Legislation has been introduced in both the Assembly and State Senate to outlaw Native American symbols in the 22 State school districts that currently use them, including Mishicot and Kewaunee where the logos have been used for nearly 100 years.

Much of Kewaunee's School District resides on sacred burial grounds where Indians lived for a time frame in excess of 5,000 years and who greeted Father Marquette and Louis Jolliet in 1674 at Kewaunee, aiding them in their Wisconsin and Mississippi River travels.

It now seems that some State Legislators feel that after all this time of Kewaunee and the other Districts observing and celebrating the Indian traditions and educating our students in this wonderful culture, that suddenly we are offending current Native Tribes and are politically incorrect at best or perhaps bigoted at worst and now must change. Therefore, if legislation is passed forcing involuntary change, 22 School Districts will change or be severely penalized monetarily.

Changeovers will include uniforms, literature, and even water tower repainting and will run into the millions of dollars for the affected 22 Districts and will promote much financial hardship for us as we've been told that this will be an unfunded state mandate and we'll bear 100% of the cost ourselves.

These proceedings all transpire during the time of our State's and Nation's worst fiscal crisis since the Great Depression of 1929! Wisconsin will struggle for years over the aftereffects of a 6.8 billion State Budget shortfall! Business and industrial jobs are departing the State ("Escape from Wisconsin ??!") in unprecedented numbers, severely impacting State revenue to fund essential functions such as State aid to School Districts. So why, I ask, are the Madison politicians further adding to the crisis rather than constructively seeking economic recovery and stopping the exodus of business and industry from our borders? Common sense dictates that if the Legislature mandates these changes, then the State must pay the District to effect them!

Mark G. Hinesh

Kewaunee, Wisconsin

APPENDIX 8.3

Kewaunee and Mishicot's Native American Heritage

Our two cities and school districts do in fact live on sacred grounds. Father Jacques Marquette celebrated Mass and was welcomed by the Potawatomi Indians upon landing on the Kewaunee River and Lake Michigan bluffs on November 1, 1674. Relations with the Potawatomi, who were hunters, fisherman, and crop growers, were generally good and Kewaunee (2 Indian meanings: "Where are we?" (called out in times of dense fog) and "Prairie Hen") was site of villages and burial grounds north to Ahnapee, south to Kewaunee's Carlton Township, and westward to the Tisch Mills area of Kewaunee and Manitowoc counties.

Father Marquette and Louis Jolliet soon abandoned their search quest for Cathay (China) and aided by our local Indians, explored the head waters of Green Bay, the Fox and Wisconsin River, and ultimately reached the Mississippi ("Father of Waters" of Indian Legend). They ultimately helped open "Wisconsin" (Algonquian and Ojibwa word from "wishkonsing" meaning "place of the beaver"), for hunting, trapping, logging, crop planting and spiritual ministry.

The Native American Heritage of Wisconsin is well documented in gravesites, artifacts, cave relics, and moraines extending from 600 years prior to the white man's first North American explorations to perhaps 5000 years or more. Quite a cultural legacy have the Indians left us!

Most of us farmers, construction workers and all who work in our precious soil have dug up Native American artifacts such as pottery, harvesting and meal preparation tools, hunting items such as hatchets, arrowheads, tomahawks and knives, and recreational items such as ceremonial smoking pipes, drums, turtle shells, tom-toms and headdresses with feathers. Many of these aforementioned items are on display at the Kewaunee Public Library.

We of the Kewaunee and Mishicot School Districts have for decades celebrated with great reverence and dignity our Native American heritages by adopting with pride our school logo's of "Indians". We do not use human caricatures in war dress. We do not use warfare items like spears and tomahawks to depict combat (such as the Atlanta Braves Baseball Franchise with "The Tomahawk Chop") or the Florida State Seminoles using a spear thrown to intimidate their opponents at football games. We do not use degrading caricatures such as the Washington Football "Redskins" with war feathers and weapons on helmets or "Chief Wahoo" of the Cleveland Baseball Indians with a degradingly large hook nose and buck teeth.

Kewaunee's football helmet sports simply a "Flying K". Mishicot uses a standard "M". Kewaunee's basketball uniforms have a ceremonial feathered headdress on the right leg. This is celebratory only and does not depict combat, unlike the pro sports teams.

Both Kewaunee and Mishicot school systems have for decades used uniforms with similar great sensitivity and decency while celebrating what our treasured Native American history has to offer. Our schools systems have not "crossed the line" into political insensitivity or bigotry as has been recently alleged by certain elements of A.I.M. (American Indian Movement) and news media who have influenced the beginning of legislation in the State Senate and Assembly designed to outlaw all "Indian" references in our school systems under penalty of stiff fines and forfeitures. These special interest groups seek to deprive us of our rights to tastefully celebrate our historical heritage while themselves turning a "blind eye" to the big moneyed interests and high priced lawyers of the NFL, MLB, and big time university's who do as they please. That, I say, is where the political insensitivity and bigotry truly lies, not with our local school districts, which are doing their best to instill historical pride and good citizenship in our most precious resources...... our children. What about their rights?

The Mishicot School District even has a legal compact with Lower Michigan tribal descendants of Chief Mishicot of many years past. This includes their right to use a "Woods Indian" (fur cap with single feather) on water towers and Indian logos within their school system. So I ask, is that also to be "null and voided" by a rush to judgment in the Wisconsin State Legislature under siege by a vocal relatively few, plus news media, starved for controversial stories?

And, who pays for the thousands of dollars of uniform change-overs? State aids? No way! It was simply another unfunded State mandate, paid out of the pockets of the local school district taxpayer.

Where are our rights to tastefully continue to celebrate our heritages in the Kewaunee and Mishicot school districts? Of the many students and parents I've talked to in both Districts, continuance of the "status quo" appears to be in the 90+ percent range. It is hardly a mandate for change. Kewaunee and Mishicot folks need to decide our logo's on our own. We've offended no one, after all these years. Please write your Representatives in Madison before another precious heritage, is forever lost, all in the name of "political correctness."

Mark G. Hinesh

First Senate District

Kewaunee, Wisconsin

Memo to Senator Alan J. Lasee

May 5, 2009

Dear Alan,

I called at your office in Madison and was advised to send this additional material to your home address.

It's very material to the historical article I wrote in that it shows active ongoing involvement of the Kewaunee School District in Native American Culture and the actual human representation we use (an elderly patriarch, not a hostile warrior).

Is there any way you can reproduce this and attach it to my letter? I think it has the potential to be very convincing evidence to our cause, namely to retain our Native American traditions within the Kewaunee, Mishicot, and other school districts and other school districts statewide who use them.

If called upon to testify and further explain our positions on this pending legislation, I would ask my good friend and fellow 1963 classmate, Glenn Teske, to accompany me to Madison. We would bring along Kewaunee sports uniforms to show the extent of our representations and explain how we have located burial sites of two Indian chiefs (buried upright to watch over their tribes) in the Tisch Mills area of the Kewaunee School District.

Meanwhile I'll appear before the Mishicot District on May 6 and encourage letter writing to the Legislature and Governor and explain the need to retain our historical culture. I'll do the same at Kewaunee High School next week. We just can't lose this right for our children to decide!

Thank you for your assistance and support.

Sincerely,

Mark Hinesh

APPENDIX 8.5

In Retrospect:

Unless we mount a serious letter-writing campaign <u>NOW</u> to Senator Lasee, Representative Bies, and Governor Doyle, this right to retain our Native American cultural ties will be lost forever... time draws short.

Yet two days ago, a Maryland Federal District Court of Appeals reaffirmed the rights of the Washington Redskins NFL team to all their logo's and mascots, much of which is insensitive. Certainly a dual standard is at work here: they keep theirs... we lose ours when all we are trying to do is to celebrate our wonderful Native American heritage from great people who were stewards of the land, the waters and the total environment in which they lived, protected and respected for thousands of years prior to the arrival of our ancestors. Please let us learn to celebrate Wisconsin's Native American past...and not be forced to discard and forget it.

Mark Hinesh

Kewaunee Class of 1963

From the Office of: Agricultural Heritage & Resources Inc.
N2251 State Road 42, Kewaunee, WI 54216
Phone: 920-388-0604 Fax: 920-388-0192 E-mail at: ahr@itol.com
Visit us on the Web at: wisconsinruralheritage.org
Committed to preserving agriculture's diverse heritage and promoting its future

December 23, 2007

Agricultural Heritage Resources, Inc. has received a wonderful donation from Mark G. Hinesh. He has donated 144 (2 were doubles, numbers 91 and 98) toy tractors and other toy vehicles (see attached appraisal) having to do with farm work.

Mark Hinesh is helping AHR in achieving their mission statement of preserving our heritage, past, present, and future.

Jennifer Gozdzialski
Director of Acquisitions

NOTES

Agent Orange

Agent Orange is the code name for one of the herbicides and defoliants used by the U.S. military as part of its herbicidal warfare program. During the Vietnam War, between 1962 and 1971, the United States military sprayed over 12,000,000 US gallons of chemical herbicides and defoliants in Vietnam, eastern Laos and parts of Cambodia, as part of a program's goal was to defoliate forested and rural land and depriving guerrillas of cover and rural support from peasants.

Between 1965 and 1970, the United States dropped more then 50,000 tons of Agent Orange on Vietnam. By 1971, 12 percent of the total area of South Vietnam had been sprayed with defoliating chemicals, at an average concentration of 13 times the recommended United States Department of Agriculture application rate for domestic use. Exposure to Dioxin, a highly toxic substance found in Agent Orange and some other herbicides has been shown in studies to be linked to a number of cancers and other health effects in humans.

The Green Berets

In the United States the Green Berets is a popular name for the United States Army Special Forces. The United States Army describe Special Forces (SF), as an elite, multi-purpose force for high priority operational targets of strategic importance, and that wearing the green beret of the SF has a demanding intensive and rigorous training. Selection requires high standards of physical fitness and academic ability. The SF linage history of unconventional warfare dates back more than 200 years.

TET Offensive

On January 31 1968 during the TET holiday which is celebrated in Vietnamese Society for several days as a time to visit family and friends, the North Vietnamese Army (NVA) and the Viet Cong (VC) made massive and coordinated attacks through out South Vietnam. The NVA/VC expected that the people of South Vietnam would join them and overthrow the government of South Vietnam. This did not happen and the NVA/VC sustained huge losses of life at the mercy of the firepower of superior American forces and South Vietnamese Army.

Vietnamese Demilitarized Zone (DMZ)

The **Vietnamese Demilitarized Zone (DMZ)** was established by the First Indochina War as a dividing line between North and South Vietnam. During the Second Indochina War (known as the Vietnam War) the DMZ became important as the battleground demarcation separating North Vietnamese territory from South Vietnamese territory.

West Point

The United States Military Academy at West Point is a four-year coeducational federal service academy located at West Point, New York. Over a thousand cadets enter each year as officers-in-training. Their tuition is fully funded by the Army in exchange for an active duty service obligation upon graduation. Graduates are commissioned as second lieutenants.

ABOUT THE AUTHOR

Mark G. Hinesh grew up on a fifth generation small dairy farm in Wisconsin and was educated in a one room elementary school. He attended Kewaunee High School and graduated in 1963. In 1967 he graduated from the Army Reserve Officers' Training Corps and business administration program at St. Norbert College. He was awarded 4 Bronze Stars, the Army Commendation Medal and Vietnamese Special Forces Parachute Wings and the Cross of Gallantry while serving as a Captain with Army Special Forces in Vietnam and Cambodia (1969 – 1971).

The content of this autobiographical work spans over sixty years, from the middle of the 20th century and into the 21st. Of special interest are the recollections of his wartime experience in the Green Berets in Vietnam.

He worked for many years as a Sheriff Officer. He has been a caregiver for family and others for the past forty years. His activities in the social life of his community are extensive and reflect his positive approach that happiness and joy should be shared by all. As part of his volunteer work he has personally funded the development of a new sports center.

Mark G. Hinesh can be contacted by email at:

mark.hinesh@pacificacademic.com

55430921R00082

Made in the USA
Charleston, SC
26 April 2016